Influencers

STEPPING OUT
IN BOLDNESS

WOMEN EMPOWERING OTHER WOMEN

Compiled By

Dr. Valarie W. Harris

Dana D. Wilson   Kristina Truell   Dr. Maxine Collins   Dr. Myria D. Thompson

Renita M. Courtney   Tara D. Henry   Dr. Yvonne Smith-Jones

Influencers Stepping Out in Boldness: Women Empowering Other Women

Copyright © 2023 Dr. Valarie Williams Harris

* * *

Published by:
Stepping Out with Purpose, LLC
steppingout@talktimeval.com

Anthology Editor
Chandra Sparks Splond, M.S.E.
www.chandrasparkssplond.com

Book Layout and Design
DHBonner Virtual Solutions, LLC
www.dhbonner.net

ISBN for Paperback: 979-8-9877190-0-8
ISBN for Hardback: 979-8-9877190-1-5
ISBN for eBook: 979-8-9877190-2-2

Printed in the United States of America

Dedicated to every individual, author, educator, leader, creator, trainer, speaker, and entrepreneur who reads this book. Don't allow the noise or distractions to stop you from being the influencer willing to step out boldly for such a time as this. People are waiting on you.

Table of Contents

Influencers

STEPPING OUT
IN BOLDNESS

WOMEN EMPOWERING OTHER WOMEN

Introduction

Have you ever wondered about the impact you have had on the lives of others? In this journey called life, you have and will encounter many people—those who will influence you, some known and unknown—who you will influence.

A young woman lost her parents at an early age and would have never thought in a million years that she would be instrumental in saving many lives. The young woman was such an influencer that she was chosen out of many other beautiful girls to marry a king. Then a time came when the young woman needed to make a request before the king that would be on behalf of her people. The king loved her so much that he was willing to give her half of his kingdom.

In the process of speaking before the king, she influenced her people to fast, and without any hesitation, they all agreed. As an influencer, she stepped out boldly to save her people regardless of the circumstances she might have faced in the process. Who am I talking about? I am so glad you asked. I am talking about the Bible character Queen Esther. There have been women for centuries who were influencers who stepped out boldly to serve and help others. What we do as women can't be solely about ourselves. Esther impacted those who met her during various encounters, preparation, and circumstances in the book of Esther.

As you read the chapters introduced in this anthology, know that your destiny includes your intended influence on those you have met and will meet throughout your lifetime. God created you to be an influencer. Say out loud right now: *I am an influencer!* He created you to make a difference and to impact the lives of those you meet daily, so don't be afraid to let your light so shine before men. What you have inside of you has aided you in being the person others look to for advice, empathy, compassion, and love because of how they have seen you show care toward others.

As the visionary author of *Influencers Stepping Out in Boldness*, I pray that you will make a conscious effort to willingly listen, encourage, inspire, and empower others by letting them know they matter. You can influence others by giving them hope that they can make it through obstacles and the challenging times we live in today. Be that motivator people need to help them step out boldly to believe in themselves, allowing God to do the rest.

—Dr. Valarie W. Harris, *Visionary Author*

The Influencer's Pathway

DR. VALARIE W. HARRIS

In this fast-paced society, longevity in education is in question. According to recent studies, on average about fifty percent of teachers say they would quit teaching now. Many fear the unknown and the lack of support, and most question whether it is worth being a teacher.

My career as a teacher started when I was twenty-three years old. The uncertainties that crossed my mind caused me to wonder whether I was in the right profession because, after all, I started off as a business major and changed my course of study to become a teacher. As the years kept passing by, I realized that teaching, training, equipping, and creating was my niche. The excitement of teaching grew stronger and stronger because I learned how to adapt my teaching skills so that my students could learn.

Everyone has a different learning style, and some people learn at a faster pace than others. Once I grasped that concept, creative ideas flooded my mind on how I would help my students be successful. The delight of exposing them to many things became enjoyable.

Fortunately, I was blessed to work and collaborate with a group of women and men who felt the same way I did about the students we worked with. We did many things together for the benefit of our students—picnics, pool parties, and trips to various states. We exposed our students to many places and activities they had never experienced before. They learned the importance of working on a job. A lot of times, we had to encourage each other to keep our sanity. We fought many battles together, mended many fences, and overcame many obstacles that came against us. Even through some of the setbacks, we made it through because of the grace of God.

Stepping out in boldness takes time. It does not happen overnight. It is a process in which you will need to take small steps in the various fields you might find yourself in that prepare you for the different stages of your life. Looking back, I remember a time when computers or technology were of no interest to me. However, one of my co-teachers had come into teaching from the industry side of the spectrum and was computer and technologically savvy. Believe it or not, I had a computer in my classroom that I had not planned to use. She said to me, "Val, are you going to use that computer?"

I remember telling her no. Then I proceed to tell her she could have it to use in her classroom. Nonetheless, she did not stop persisting in influencing me and helped me realize I needed to learn how to use that computer. After all, I was a business major first and could type fast on a regular old type-writer. Why did I need to know how to use a computer?

Guess what? Today, I can do all kinds of things with the use of a computer. Why am I saying all of this to you? Sometimes we are our worse enemy because we limit ourselves and miss out on things that will benefit us in the future. She was such an influencer in my life that we went back to school and obtained our master's degrees from Virginia Tech University.

Our connections to people are an important aspect of our lives that can change the trajectory of our mindset. Try not to be close-minded to things you are not familiar with. Yes, life as a teacher has its ups and downs, but overall, if it is your passion to serve and equip others making the decision to endure hard times in the process is worth it.

Learning things, you don't understand can lead to other fantastic opportunities. Four other people influenced my career as a teacher, which led me to become certified by the University of Virginia in the areas of technology. It started a ripple effect to becoming the webmaster at my school, the lead teacher for technology, one of the coordinators of a work program, and the transition specialist who served the faculty, community, parents, and many students. Let me tell you, these women were great at what they did as principals and administrators during their time in education. They loved working with people and were effective in everything they did for the children, teachers, or whomever they encountered. Unfortunately, everyone you meet in the field of education you will not connect with, but make sure you learn with whom you can collaborate will not stab you in the back in the process. Even when it seems dismal, those you will meet and encounter, never doubt that God is still in control of your destiny. The weapon might form, but it will not prosper (Isaiah 54:17).

Over the past years, I have experienced many people through the numerous vocations and leadership roles in which I've functioned, yet I never really thought of myself as an influencer during the process. My focus was to effectively impact the lives of my family, friends, co-workers, students, church, community, and educational and social environments. That is why working diligently to be a positive role model for my children and the students I taught for more than thirty-four years was important. Did I always get it right? No. Did I make mistakes along the way? Yes, I did, but I continued striving to do my best on any task. As Maya Angelou once said, "People will forget what you said. People will forget what you did, but people will never forget how you made them feel."

THE INFLUENCER'S LEADERSHIP ROLE

An influencer exerts influence, inspires, and guides the behavior and actions of others, and leadership means to influence and serve others. How amazing is that? So, being an influencer in any field is about serving others by inspiring, encouraging, guiding, and giving them the expectancy of success. As we look at Matthew 20:26, 28 NLT, it teaches us that we lead by serving and serve by leading. "Anyone wanting to be a leader among you must be your servant." The following list of authors gives insight into the topic of leadership:

- Warren Bennis, a scholar, consultant, and author who is regarded as a pioneer in leadership states, "Leadership is the capacity to translate vision into reality" (Sohn, 2014).

- Bill Gates, a business magnate, software developer, investor, and philanthropist who is best known as the co-founder of Microsoft, says, "As we look ahead into the next century, leaders are those who empower others" (Gates, 2009).

- Peter Northouse, a professor, consultant, lecturer on the trends in leadership research, and author, attributes leadership as "A process whereby an individual influences a group of individuals to achieve a common goal" (Northouse, 2021).

Similarly, each definition agreed with the bestselling author, speaker, and pastor who has written many books focusing on leadership. John Maxwell said, "Leadership is influence, nothing more, nothing less" (Maxwell, J. C., 2010). As discussed above, leaders have the responsibility to develop others. Believe it or not, we influence people daily, whether in our home, on our job, in our church, or in our community. Influence can be observed in a leader's foresight as he inspires others to succeed. Leadership embraces multiple meanings with various descriptions.

Know this: Your leadership carries a heavy mantle no matter what field you work in; it is essential. There is a great need for those in leadership who know how to treat those they work with in a positive, caring way. At times, we all struggle with various things, but it does not give anyone the right to manipulate or degrade those you work with. We struggle to make it in our society, and it's time for those in leadership to stop mishandling those they work with. People know when you are not authentic with them, even if they don't say it. Your positive influence is a must if you want people to flourish. Your intentions and motives as a leader need to be God motivated. Our world needs mending and healing. It is so important that we as leaders pray for those we lead daily.

Jesus was the best model of a leader who exhibited practical skills. He possesses effective skills and demonstrates prayer's role in a leader's life. One of His essential purposes for visiting the earth was to serve and save the lost. In doing so, He showed what moral and ethical values looked like in a leader. I made it for thirty-four-plus years in teaching with prayer being a part of my life. I wouldn't have lasted that long if Jesus was not a part of my life.

Why am I saying this? I want to encourage whoever is reading this right now that whatever profession you are in, God is our source—the source who can keep us from failing, who can keep us from giving up. If you are at the point of giving up, please talk with Jesus who will and can steer you back on the right path.

THE INFLUENCER'S DAILY LIFESTYLE

Leaders communicate their daily life in three different areas. They display it publicly, privately, and personally. Their public life is when they interact with people at work, in the community, and through social gatherings at church or other types of events. They must present themselves in a manner that represents authenticity. As leaders, people watch us everywhere we go. One must be mindful of his actions and the way he communicates with others. According to James 1:19 ESV, *"Know this, my beloved brothers: let every person be quick to hear, slow to speak, slow to anger."* One must remember that people are evaluating and sizing us up constantly.

Dale Roach, a popular pastor, consultant, leadership, and team development instructor proposes, "How one lives is the foundation for what he or she believes" (Roach, 2016).

In the private life of a leader, one must be careful whom he allows in his inner circle. Of course, most of his circle will include his family and a few selected friends. Looking at Jesus's life, He dealt with His family and friends with whom He lived among. Before He chose His twelve disciples as referenced in Luke 6:12–13 ESV, He prayed first before He selected them. Jesus's actions indicate that we must be mindful of the friends we surround ourselves with, making sure they are followers of Christ. I do believe that as a leader, prayer should play a vital part in your daily life.

A leader's personal life should model doing what is right in the eyes of those you encounter, whether it is behind closed doors, public or private. Our personal life should demonstrate how we treat our family, our friends, and even a stranger we might meet. We should show who we are by living out God's purpose as we serve others continuously.

THE INFLUENCER INSIDE OF YOU

Influencers value themselves and others. They exhibit a consistent attitude toward their family, job, ministry, personal and professional development, finances, health practices, and community, even when things might not be going their way.

They know how to empower others to move forward to success in their lives. They are good listeners and communicators. They have a real zeal and passion for what they do to help others to be effective.

Look at yourself in the mirror. The influencer who resides inside of you should display these attributes. If you can relate to any of the characteristics listed, put a 0, 1, 2, or 3 beside the response. Zero you don't relate at all, 1 means you kind of relate, 2 somewhat relate, and 3 definitely relate.

1. **Inspire** others to step up and step out of their comfort zone. ___
2. **Network** by building relationships with others. ___
3. A **follower** who submits willingly. ___
4. A **lifestyle** of honesty and respect toward others. ___
5. **Unique** abilities. ___
6. **Equipped** to push others to fulfill their purpose. ___
7. **Noteworthy** of their responsibilities. ___
8. **Collaborate** with a team to reach potential goals. ___
9. **Enthusiastic** about unlocking hidden potential. ___
10. **Respected** by family, friends, and co-workers. ___

Use this scale to score yourself:

0–10: Work-in-Progress Influencer
11–20: Stepping Forward Influencer
21–30: Soaring Influencer

Can you relate to the influencer who resides inside you waiting to lift others out of despair, worthlessness, and not feeling they matter? Know this: You are an influencer who people are waiting on to help overcome the obstacles and challenges that plague so many today. Remember that you have what it takes to draw people from feeling less than to empower them to see they are enough and already have the victory, but they must believe it for themselves.

The influencer inside you has what it takes to speak a thing, and it will happen. The influencer inside of you is victorious and ready to explore new opportunities. The influencer inside of you is willing to embrace change. The influencer inside of you knows what it takes to be laser-focused. As an influencer, you have the power to positively influence others to make a difference in the world we live in. It is about being your authentic self with whatever you are involved in doing.

An influencer who steps out in boldness as a leader is essential because they can help promote positive change, be an advocate, inspire others, and create a lifelong learning and growth culture. They are passionate about their work and are committed to positively impacting the lives of their students and other audiences. They can use their platform to share their knowledge, advocate for change, and build community; they can make a meaningful impact on the education industry and the lives of students and educators alike.

THE INFLUENCER'S TRANSFORMATION CYCLE

As an influencer, stepping out in boldness does not mean that your life has always been on an easy street. We all face challenges while teaching, training, equipping, inspiring, encouraging, and empowering others. It's all a part of the game of life. That's why I want to leave you with some real-life stories and struggles that you can face, even when you, step by step, move past your fears and step out of your comfort zone to boldly pursue your dreams, passions, and purpose as you unlock your hidden potential.

Being an influencer has its challenges, but those challenges have shaped and molded me into who I am today, for a time such as this. These stories will include life lessons and experiences that will help you through whatever you are going through in your life right now. Transitioning through the life cycles you encounter daily is real. Understand that it is a process everyone experiences. I gained humility along with a transformed growth mindset. The cycles that will be mentioned include spiritual, family, career, health and wellness, financial, living environment, and personal and professional growth. All these components play an essential role in the life of an influencer. Each cycle has its different responsibility in your life daily. They are all intertwined with each other. Look with me at the cycle our lives are centered around.

SPIRITUAL LIFE

As I grew in education and leadership, I had to learn how to bring stability to my life. I realized I needed a closer relationship with God because I had no problem telling anyone what I had on my mind if I felt they were out of order with me. So spiritually, I needed to be refueled in this area and made a conscious effort to spend more time in prayer and studying the Word. After all, I had grown up in the church but strayed away. My reactions to the different things I experienced caused a shift in my mindset. Only I could step out and allow God to direct my path. From that point on, something changed in my life. As time passed, I continued to grow spiritually, and after retiring from teaching, God called me to preach the Gospel, and I received my license in 2013.

Since this book will explore various avenues from many perspectives, this was surely a bold step in my life when this happened. According to Psalm 37:23 NIV, *"The LORD makes firm the steps of the one who delights in him."* Daily I ask God to order my steps.

If you are undergoing problems or struggling to make it through the hard times, you might want to spend some time in the presence of God. He is our source. He is our refuge and strength in the time of trouble. He will deliver you from whatever you are going through. If you need help in any area of your life, there is nothing wrong with reaching out for help if you need it. There is a time in all our lives when we must yield our will to God's will for our lives.

FAMILY LIFE

As parents, you often try to do your best to raise your family with good values and ethics by teaching them right from wrong. At the same time, you are growing up yourself, especially if you are a young parent. It's trial and error when raising children. Sometimes we get it right, and sometimes we don't. It is essential to constantly have your teaching hat on at home, giving your children opportunities for socialization and learning social skills, which can be necessary for personal and professional development success. Our family must be one of the most critical aspects of our lives. We must constantly let our children and spouse know that we love them. We must remember that our family will keep us grounded, and they can provide us with a sense of emotional security and support, which can help when dealing with the stresses of everyday life.

Sometimes we have to say no to things that interfere with family time because through it all, our family is one of the longest-lasting relationships we can have. It is important that we cherish every moment that we get to spend with our loved ones.

HEALTH AND WELLNESS

Many times in life, people struggle with various health issues. The reason I mention this is because I had begun to have health problems. When I became ill, the doctors did not know what was wrong with me. Making a bold change was what I had to do for myself. At times, we are our worst enemy, especially if we indulge in overeating the wrong foods, overdrinking, and smoking. All these things are harmful to our bodies. Listen, I had an issue with them all. Thank God for deliverance. It is our decision to make the change. When you suffer from various illnesses, it can cause mental health issues. Ultimately, it can be the onset of emotional and physical stress, depression, low self-esteem, and a feeling of unworthiness.

A changed mindset will improve your mental health and well-being, which will help you overcome these problems encountered. It was important that I trusted God through the process. Nonetheless, I needed to do my part. Making a conscious effort to change my eating habits brought the need to begin exercising regularly and praying that God would deliver me from smoking cigarettes, and He did.

Well, I had dealt with all these illnesses for years. Once the deliverance happened, I gained more confidence and clarity and felt better mentally and physically. It is about taking charge of your life. If you are struggling with whatever it might be, I am here to tell you that you can overcome any obstacle that comes your way. You must seek help, believe, and you will benefit from God's deliverance.

FINANCIAL LIFE

Starting young in any profession can be overwhelming until you get settled about your work, especially when you are now on your own as an adult. You are spreading your wings and experiencing meeting new people and learning who you can trust. You must become responsible and financially stable to pay rent, your phone bill, and your light bill for the first time, not realizing you need a budget. It can truly put you in a dilemma. You are out there spending more money than you make. You are running up all kinds of credit cards, paying your bills late, which will cause you to have bad credit. You learn real fast that a budget is essential to wholesome living.

These are the struggles and experiences many people, including myself, have had until they come to the realization of understanding the importance of being good stewards of your money. I am sharing this with you because if you don't take control of your spending, it can lead to going deeper and deeper into debt, not knowing exactly when it happened, but it happened.

Becoming financially secure will give you the freedom and independence to pursue your dreams and goals. Having a lot of debt will keep you in bondage. It will make you feel like there is nowhere to turn until you consciously try to reduce your debt. There is nothing wrong with going to a financial planner who can help you make better decisions on your spending practice. If you don't have a financial planner, I suggest you get one. They are experts at helping you learn how to lower your debt, which will eliminate financial stress. Practicing good financial habits can improve your credit score, providing you with better credit for loans and many other avenues. That will help you accumulate wealth and achieve your financial goals.

In the process of lowering your debt, there is nothing wrong with getting a part-time job. It is a great way to start having other streams of income.

LIVING ENVIRONMENT

Have you ever wondered how people achieve success even when they have experienced many struggles? They can succeed because of determination. Being an only child can be challenging, but you learn to adapt. We lived in the projects until I finished college. Living in the projects gave me a different perspective on life and how to treat people. Yes, family during that time stuck together, looked out for one another, and if you did something wrong, the neighbor would tell your parent. My mother and father instilled in me the core values of working hard to do your best, helping others, showing love toward others, and treating people with respect, even when they did not respect you back.

Neither had a high school diploma, but they were faithful to their jobs. My father was a rigger for NASA, and my mother was a seafood worker. My parents are the reason I went to college to further my education. The determination to succeed was inside me at an early age. No matter the struggle or obstacle, I continued to step forward in my dreams and aspirations.

Oftentimes, I wondered why I was so business savvy. My grandfather owned the neighborhood grocery store and an oil delivery business. Where did all the influence of education come from? Other family members were teachers, administrators, and school counselors. Our living environment and surroundings profoundly affect who we are and why we react to certain things, our character, and our behavior. Unfortunately, it is up to us to use what we learn, positively or negatively. Sorry to say, but it is our choice. We can't blame others for the way we turn out.

Firsthand, I've experienced what bereavement can do to a family and how it disrupts plans, dreams, and future endeavors. It is up to you to turn things around for good. Once I lost my mother early in life, I fell into a state of depression, worthlessness, and hopelessness. It can be an easy slope to fall into in the loss of a loved one. Thank God for those who prayed for me during these trying times. I was able to overcome this adversity and was able to finish my college degree. Where you start in life does not determine your destination.

PERSONAL AND PROFESSIONAL GROWTH

What is the best way to improve your personal and professional growth and productivity at work as a leader? You can improve your personal and professional productivity by setting attainable goals daily, managing your time, making a list of priorities, learning to say no, being laser focused, completing one task at a time, taking numerous breaks, and eliminating distractions. Again, as an influencer, you must balance and manage your tasks to meet success. Most importantly, remember that you need self-care, plenty of rest, and plenty of water. Time in nature, listening to soft music, and reading will improve your personal growth,

Being open to obtaining additional training, taking classes, and getting certified in a different area of expertise will help you to be more persistent in pursuing your dreams, desires, and passions while stepping out on purpose as you assist others to do the same. Continuously, I took classes, obtained several degrees, and recently received my doctoral degree. It is vital to keep an open mind and become a lifelong learner. Know that whatever you do to improve yourself, you will use your gifts, talents, skills, and innovations to help the next person.

As I close this chapter, I want to encourage, inspire, and empower those who read it to understand that you are an influencer. You have greatness inside of you that the world needs. Many people who have profoundly influenced my life will never know it. Like the people you have affected, you will never know, but don't stop being the influencer with the willingness to step out in boldness to help give hope and encouragement to the people who will come into your life. Dream big and never stop pushing past whatever obstacle may come your way.

You have what it takes to make it. I am a living example of what God can do through you to help mold and shape others to succeed. For more than fifty-seven years, I have worked in diverse professions, and I pray that I have inspired and influenced people's lives because I still have much more to do to help the next generation.

ABOUT THE AUTHOR

Dr. Valarie is a wife, mother, grandmother, great-grandmother, preacher, teacher, psalmist, workshop facilitator, author, empowerment coach, business consultant, and speaker. Her greatest desire is to seek God's face and see others in the body of Christ grow into an intimate relationship with the living Savior.

Dr. Valarie is the director of ministries at her church and the founder and CEO of Stepping Out with Purpose Coaching & Consulting Company. As a leader in her church, she strives to develop lifelong learners, equipping them with the necessary resources to go to the next level and bring about a growth mindset in their leadership roles for coming generations. As an empowerment coach, her mission is to equip, empower, and inspire women in leadership and entrepreneurs to build a business that creates financial freedom and a healthy lifestyle and leave a legacy for future generations.

She is the author of six books. Her first book is a forty-day journal called *Talk Time with God; Unleashed Power of Prayer: Teens and Young Adults' Prayer Journal Workbook; Stepping Up & Stepping Out: Journal Experience; The Effects of Prayer in the Life of a Leader;* co-author of *PEARLS;* and the visionary and co-author of *Influencers Stepping Out in Boldness.* These books contain journaling exercises, stories, wisdom, and various interactive activities.

I Have Plans for You

DR. MAXINE COLLINS

"For I know the thoughts that I think toward you, saith the LORD, thoughts of peace, and not of evil, to give you an expected end."
-Jeremiah 29:11

I heard this scripture spoken in my spirit at one of the lowest times in my life, and it has truly blessed me over the years. I believe that hearing this word was the beginning of my walking in boldness. This all occurred right after I left my job. At that time, I had no other job prospects, no money in the bank, and no other source of income. But I knew I had made the right decision in leaving that job. As soon as I put in my notice, it was as if a weight was lifted from my shoulders, and I felt a sense of peace, although as time went on, the peace began to dissipate, and despair began to rear its ugly head. That is when this scripture became my anchor.

I was sitting on the bedroom floor next to my bed, looking out of the window, and praying to the Most High to show me what to do next. Suddenly, I heard in my spirit (not an audible voice), *"I know the plans that I have toward you... to give you an expected end."* At that time in my life, I was not as familiar with scripture, but I knew enough to know it was the Lord speaking to me and not me speaking to myself. I ran to my computer to look up the scripture reference and context. This would be my first true experience hearing the Word of Yah, and it blessed me immensely.

I have since learned that our spiritual proximity or connection to Yah will determine what and how we hear His voice.

Even though I still had no job or money, for some reason, after that encounter, I felt peace, and I felt a boldness like never before, a boldness to trust Yah, no matter what.

That all occurred more than fifteen years ago, and the Lord has never failed me. I have been employed with a good company for more than fifteen years. I enjoy my job and the people I work with. I later went back to school and obtained my second bachelor's degree, this one in religious education (my first bachelor's degree is in business management). I then went further later and received a master's degree in human services/marriage and family counseling, training in mental health as a qualified mental health professional—children, a certification in mental health first aid, started a nonprofit organization called Advocate Enterprises, and my doctorate in theology. I attribute this all to that one scripture that inspired me to trust Yah, get up, and walk in the boldness of His Word. I know now that the Lord was telling me to get off the floor and get busy doing what He called me to do.

Some years later, after having this revelatory experience, I did an in-depth Hebrew study on Jeremiah 29:11 around the words *expected end*. Some translations use *future* instead of *expected end*. The Hebrew word used there is *Achariyth,* and it means the last or end, hence, the future; also *posterity* (last, latter), *end* (time), *hinder* (utter) *-most, length, posterity, remnant, residue, reward.*

I like the word *posterity* in this definition because it means an individual's descendants. I believe the Lord is saying, *"Not only am I going to bring you out of your situation, but I have your children, grandchildren, and great-grandchildren in mind as well.*" I believe this to be true in my life because of a prophecy I received years later about the salvation of my daughter and grandchildren. So, when I learned the Hebraic meaning of the words *expected end* or *future,* it added more meaning to what the Lord is doing in my life. Not only is he going to protect and provide for me and show me His plan, but because I take Him at His word, He is going to protect and provide for my posterity because my daughter and grandchildren are my future.

This revelation is not only for me, but I believe it is for anyone who takes Yah at His word and walks it out in boldness.

PURPOSE AND VISION

Purpose Activates Vision

Once a person truly believes in Yah, they are normally inspired to walk in their purpose and vision unless fear and doubt set in. One thing I have learned is that when fear comes, she brings her ugly sister doubt along as well. This is when it is paramount to remember that you have not been given the spirit of fear but of power, and of love, and of a sound mind (2 Timothy 1:7). This is also the time when we are to use the Word to tell fear and doubt where to get off. This can only occur when we truly know who we are.

To be successful in the Kingdom, you must know your purpose and have a clear vision of where you are going or how to proceed. This is not always an easy task to discern. Your purpose is what you were created to do, and your vision is how you see yourself doing it. According to Dr. Myles Munroe (*The Principles and Power of Vision,* 2014), a vision is a conception that is inspired by God in the heart of a human. Also, he goes further in saying that true vision is the ability to see farther than your eyes can look (pg. 17). This means we as believers should be able to see spiritually the unlimited possibilities available to us rather than what we see through our natural eyes. We should be the ones who walk by faith and not by sight.

Many people have asked me, "How do I find my purpose?"

I believe when you find Yah, you will find your purpose—our purpose is in Him. Many overlook that because they are searching for their meaning to life through worldly desires. But to be specific, I've learned the simplest way to find your meaning for life and get started on your journey is to discover what it is that angers or bothers you the most in life. I don't mean the kind of anger that makes you want to physically fight, but the kind that urges you to get involved in seeing change occur and motivates you to move into action.

For instance, maybe you hate seeing people being taken advantage of or seeing people walking in fear, doubt, and worry rather than living their true purpose. For me, I hate for people to believe the lies of the enemy. That's why I am passionate about teaching the transformative power of Yah's Word every chance I get and in any venue I am allowed.

So after you find what you are passionate about, then ask yourself if this is something you would do whether you were paid for it or not. Once you have answered these questions, get busy doing it on any level you can. Just get busy, and before you know it, you are walking in your purpose and fulfilling your destiny. When you start walking in the direction of your destiny, the whole world begins to open up to you, meaning doors will begin to open, opportunities and opposition will begin to present themselves. Be ready because when you make your plan, the enemy takes his stand. Many people have discounted this in search of their destiny, not realizing the adversary plays a part in their purpose. But remember this: He can only do what the Lord allows. It is up to you to take what He dishes out and use it as a steppingstone or a paving stone on your journey to success. When things get hard, some may say it is time to give up or take another route, and that may well be true, but listen to that still, small voice and follow its lead.

Even though the journey may seem foolish to others, don't get off track. Stay the course, remembering what He orders He pays for.

THE FOOLISHNESS OF OBEDIENCE

"But God hath chosen the foolish things of the world
to confound the wise; and God hath chosen the weak things of the
world to confound the things which are mighty."
-1 Corinthians 1:27

Walking in obedience sometimes seems foolish. It can be seen as what I call "the foolishness of obedience." Abraham is a prime example of walking in obedience—or some might say boldness—to the Word of the Lord. In Genesis 12:1–3, the Lord instructs Abraham to leave all his familiarities and follow Him. God promised Abraham as he followed Him that He would make of him a great nation, that He would bless him and curse those who cursed him. The key point here is the Lord did not exactly give Abraham a road map of where to journey. He just instructed him to go—much like the time I left my job with nothing but a knowing. To some, this seems entirely foolish, but to those who are influencers, stepping out in boldness, it is trust and obedience.

Many times, we want a road map with GPS coordinates before we step into the deep. We want to test the waters before we get in. Think about it: If the children of Israel at the parting of the Jordan River had waited to test the waters or had allowed fear to take control of them, they would have never made it over to the Promised Land. They had to step out into the deep, trusting that the Lord would be with them.

They had to put their foot in it, so to speak. I once read a commentary on Joshua 3:15-16 which purported that the river did not part until the children of Israel stepped into the water. In other words, nothing happened until they put their foot in it, which at the time must have seemed totally foolish. I believe Yah was waiting for them to trust Him enough to do something that appeared foolish before He would do something miraculous as parting the parting the Jordan River.

Most of the time we are waiting
on Yah, and Yah is waiting on us.

Now don't get me wrong, there is nothing wrong with being cautious, getting wise counsel, and making sure we are hearing correctly from the Lord, but once we hear, we need to move. We know that whatever we do in faith, the Lord will back us. Even if we are wrong but have the right heart's desire, He is still behind us showing us the right way. He just wants us to trust Him, even if it does seem foolish. Remember, He chooses the foolish things to confound the wise (1 Corinthians 1:27).

THOUGH THE FIG TREE DOES NOT BLOSSOM

Although the fig tree shall not blossom, neither shall
fruit be in the vines; the labour of the olive shall fail,
and the fields shall yield no meat; the flock shall be cut
off from the fold, and there shall be no herd in the stalls:
Yet I will rejoice in the Lord, I will joy in the God of my
salvation. The Lord God is my strength, and He will
make my feet like hinds' feet, and He will make me to
walk upon mine high places.

-Habakkuk 3:17–19

Another thing I've learned in this walk of boldness is that circumstances do not always work the way we intend for them to work out, but as true believers, we must trust the Lord in all things. In Habakkuk 3:17–19, Habakkuk declares that even though nothing seems to be going right, he is determined to rejoice in the Lord because he believes the Lord will enable him to walk on in high places, meaning the Lord will make the hard places in his life smooth. That sounds like boldness to me.

For instance, where he states that although the fig tree does not blossom, there is no fruit on the vines, the olive produce has failed and the fields yield no meat; for us this could mean that the plans we have made have produced nothing. The disappearance of the flock from the fold in this scripture could very well represent for us our savings accounts, pension, or 401(k) being depleted. Yet he declares he will rejoice in the Lord, Yahweh, because he knows that He is his salvation—his Yeshua. This is where we need to be in the midst of trials, that even though things around us are fading, we have got to know that He will make our feet like hinds' feet, meaning the feet of deer who have the ability to scale high places.

We must trust the Lord, and in doing so, we will always feel hope, even when things seem to be at their worst. Believers should never give up hope. I believe it is hope that faith attaches to in order to bring about the desired outcome. Without hope, faith has nothing to build on. The scripture says, *faith is the substance of things hoped for and the evidence of things not seen* (Hebrews 11:1). So faith consists of hope. The story of the fig tree is about trusting Yah while in the midst of struggle and doubt.

Have you ever been in a place of trusting Yah, but everything around you seems to be falling apart? Well, I want to encourage you to trust the Almighty. He is a faithful, loving Father who has an orchestrated plan for His children. The plan sometimes includes struggle, but only to build your character and faith. Our struggles are no more than purifiers.

If we were to really look at our lives in that vein, we will see that the Spirit of Yah is sustaining us through our many struggles. I often go to the Word of Yah to find comfort and answers in my times of struggle. Sure enough, the answer is there, but then it still seems to be a struggle to conform to the answer. I believe this to be true because the mind must be renewed constantly to the Word before we are transformed by it. Through all the heartaches and pain, through lost dreams and plans, through mistakes and misunderstandings, through all kinds of sufferings, it is the Spirit of Yah's Word that has sustained me. As the psalmist reminds us in Psalm 91:11, *"For He will give His angels charge over thee, to keep thee in all thy ways."*

POTENTIAL

"Now to Him who is able to do immeasurably [exceeding abundantly] more than all we ask or imagine according to the power that is at work within us."
-Ephesians 3:20

There is something very meaningful that my mother shared with me many years ago when I was struggling in my first year of college, and it still inspires me today. She told me, "If they can teach it, you can learn it." I believe what my mother was conveying to me is that I have within me the potential to do whatever I've been given the opportunity to do. This simple statement has kept me seeking purpose and vision for my life. What she was really saying is I can do all things, I have all the potential on the inside of me, and I just need to tap into it.

Everyone on planet earth has potential, which is the ability to walk out and carry out your purpose. Potential is the power within to move and do. It is inspired by vision. Think of potential in this manner: The seed of an apple has the potential of becoming an apple tree. If that seed is placed in the right soil, the right environment, and is nourished properly, it will grow into its intended function. The same is true with us. There is a seed of greatness planted in each of us, and we have the potential to become that which the Lord has purposed. He is the one who puts the seed of greatness inside of each believer, and He is the one who can bring it to fruition.

It saddens me when I see potential wasted—when I see young men and women giving up on life because of the struggles they face. They simply just do not understand that struggle is part of the journey. Every opportunity I get, I try to share this principle. I try to encourage people to see the big picture. I aspire to do this not only with the young, but there are many seasoned believers who also tend to fall for this trap of the enemy. We must take seriously the words spoken to Jeremiah (Jeremiah 29:11), that the plans the Lord has for us are good. Though we may not be called to prophesy to nations, we can prophesy to ourselves by rehearsing the promises of Yah and standing firm on what He has declared for us as His children.

We must remember that the potential that we have is directly related to the assignment the Lord has given us to fulfill. We have all that we need right on the inside of us. The problem is many are not aware of this hidden power, or they dismiss it and allow it to lie dormant. I like to say we are built for the purpose we are called to do. We have the right personality, the right stamina, the right demeanor, and all the right stuff to do and be the person we are to be. We are the answer to someone's prayer, and until we release that potential hiding behind fear and doubt, many prayers will go unanswered, and we will live an unfulfilled life.

That's not why Yeshua hung on the cross; that's not why He bled and died. He came to give us life and for us to live abundantly. Ephesians 3:20 says:

"Now to Him who is able to do immeasurably [exceeding abundantly] more than all we ask or imagine according to the power that is at work within us."

That power is potential. It can be explosive, expandable, but it should not be extinguishable. We sometimes extinguish it by not allowing our full potential to operate.

IMAGINATION

The Lord said to Abram after Lot had parted from him,
'Look around from where you are, to the north and south, to
the east and west. All the land that you see I will give to you
and your offspring forever. I will make your offspring like the
dust of the earth, so that if anyone could count the dust, then

your offspring could be counted. Go, walk through the length and breadth of the land, for I am giving it to you.'"

-Genesis 13:14–17

This scripture gives a general idea of imagination. Abram had to use his imagination to see in his spirit what Yahweh was showing him. Our imagination is a powerful tool we can use to achieve the vision and purpose Yah places in our hearts. If you can in some way imagine it, you will achieve it. In other words, if you can see it in your spirit, you can manifest it.

Believing is the process of seeing by the spirit of Yah. It is trusting the faith-filled words of Yah, by seeing the manifestation of it in the spirit. The scripture says as a man thinks in his heart, so is he (Proverbs 23:7). Where you find yourself next year will be the result of what you imagine or believe for yourself today. The Word tells us to cast down imagination that exalts itself above the Lord. This means we need to get rid of the negative, downgrading thoughts that can overtake our mind.

These thoughts have been coined the phrase ANTs—Automatic Negative Thoughts—by Dr. Daniel Amen, a well-known doctor and neuroscientist who studies brain scans for his research. ANTs are the thoughts that have been bombarding our minds, and unbeknownst to us, they are destroying the plans that the Lord has for us.

We must fuel our imagination by destroying those ANTs. The only way to do this is by applying the Word of Yah to every situation. When a problem arises in our lives, we must choose what the Lord says about it and go from there. For instance, what does the Lord say about healing, the lack of peace and joy, or the presence of anxiety? The scripture is full of the answers that we can simply apply to receive the manifestation of the desired result. But not only that, we should also examine ourselves. The Lord wants only the best for us, but we must also admit when we've missed the mark and get back in alignment in order to hear from Yah and receive the blessing.

Another aspect of imagination is that it takes faith to work. It takes faith to move what you see in the spirit or in your imagination into the natural realm. In other words, it's going to take faith to take that which you see in your mind and move it to the natural realm, thereby making it tangible. For example, if you say you believe but you do not apply faith to what you say you believe, your faith is dead and yields no manifestation. Faith without works is considered dead faith (James 2:14–26).

I've heard it said, if you can't see it in your imagination or your spirit, you cannot have it. I believe this to be a true analogy of the power of our imagination. But, I can hear a few of you thinking now, *I've gotten a few good things that I didn't imagine or ingrain in my spirit. I didn't even really pray for it. I've been blessed, and I didn't do all that.* And that may be very true based on two assumptions. One, maybe the Sovereign Lord placed it on someone's heart to pray for you because it was something He needed you to have in order for you to reach your destiny. Two, you may have just been receiving crumbs from the Master's table, which is not bad at all, but for me, I would rather sit at the Master's table and receive *all* that He has for me.

The way to do this is to communicate with Him in the spirit. Take the words of your prayers and give pictures to them in your imagination; make the words real. After all, that's how He created the world, and we are created in His image, with the ability to do likewise. He saw us and then created us. In other words, we have the same power, the power to use our imagination and create. We are creators of our destiny. Give this some thought: Those who are bent on doing evil in this world use their imagination, and many are effective in bringing about evil. Then we as Believers in the Most High should be aware that we can be just as effective in bringing about good using this same principle.

We can either create using the world's way, or we can learn to create using the Word's way. The choice is ours.

Moses told the children of Israel, *"I call heaven and earth to record this day against you, that I have set before you life and death, blessing and cursing: therefore choose life, that both thou and thy seed may live"* (Deuteronomy 30:19). We have the ability with use of our Godly imagination to choose. I pray you choose life.

THE TRIBE

To become an influencer and to walk in boldness, you must have accountability partners, those in your company who are assigned to you to assist you in choosing life. I call them my tribe, which consists of several bold and successful women of Yah and two men who are bold enough to occasionally hang out with women and not be threatened, and to keep us balanced. (The two men of course are married to two of my tribal sisters.) Your tribe must be those who motivate, encourage, and push you into your destiny by holding you accountable. They are more like midwives than anything else for they are there to assist you in giving birth to your God-given desires. Just being in their very presence makes me want to come up higher.

The tribe must be those who are not envious, petty, or jealous of your success, but they see your success as their success as well. A tribe of this caliber is not a group that you put together, but one that the Lord designs specifically for you. The Father is the only one who knows the people you should have in your tribe. The people He places there may not necessarily be the kind you would generally associate with, but if you trust Yah, you will see how the least likely person will sometimes be the one who inspires you the most.

Besides having that core group of close associates—your tribe—everyone still needs a covering, especially those of us in ministry. We all need someone who has been or who is going in the direction we are striving to go. We need someone who can provide guidance and direction, comfort, and most importantly, prayer. This is someone who can serve as a spiritual counselor and assist you in your ministry. The members of the tribe are the ones who hold you accountable on what you and your spiritual counselor are working on. For instance, maybe the Lord has placed in your heart to start an international ministry. You will need someone who is already doing what you desire to do, someone who has been where you want to go.

Just as your tribe is chosen by Yah, the same is true for your spiritual covering. This person is chosen by Yah. They may or may not be your pastor or the person you think would be a suitable covering. I would encourage anyone looking for that special person to be patient and know that once He has placed this desire in your heart, He is faithful to bring it to pass. Until that person is revealed, continue walking in your journey and trusting the Lord. For after all, the Lord is our Heavenly Covering, though He has someone assigned here in the earthly realm to walk with you.

SETBACKS

"These things I have spoken to you, that in Me
you may have peace. In the world you [will have tribulation; but be
of good cheer, I have overcome the world."
-John 16:33

On this journey, there will be setbacks, but never allow the setbacks to upset you. They are there for a perfectly good reason, though the reason may not always be apparent at the time. In the passage of scripture listed, Yeshua, is encouraging us as believers not to allow trials, tribulations, hardships, or closed doors to deter us from our destiny. In other words, we should use the Word to unbury our dreams, which have been buried under life's setbacks. When hard times come, we all have had the tendency to shrink back or give up, but Yeshua is saying, "Be of good cheer. I have overcome the world. Don't allow the world to drag you down. Don't allow these setbacks to bury what I have placed in you." It is easy to allow our dreams to become covered by all the setbacks we face, but as influencers stepping out in boldness, we must learn to take the shovel of praise and uncover what the setbacks have buried. Praise and worship is what unburies the dreams and uncovers that which has been lying dormant for a while.

We must remember that the gifts, dreams, or destinies that the Lord has given us are without repentance, so He is not going to take back what He has given. We must take it back from the grave; we must take back what the hardships and pain have buried. To be successful in accomplishing this, we need to learn the art of praise and worship. Praising the Lord during hard times is not easy, so I suggest praising the Lord at all times, and when the hard times come, when the struggle becomes real, when you feel overwhelmed, praise will just flow out from you naturally.

For He promises to keep us in perfect peace whose mind is stayed on Him (Isaiah 26:3). Praising and worshiping the Lord keeps your mind on Him. This may not be the true definition of praise and worship for many, but for me, praise is the process of speaking forth the promises of Yah, lifting His name, claiming victory in His name, giving Him His accolades or His props. It is shouting from the rooftops about His wonderful and glorious love and blessings. Worship could involve some of the aforementioned statements, but for me, it is a time of receiving in my spirit that which I have been praising Him for. It is about opening my heart to hear what He is saying.

Sometimes the setbacks can strengthen our character, build our faith, and align us with the Lord's will. But by not sitting in His presence in worship, we may miss this opportunity of hearing how the Lord will use the setbacks we face. I'm sure many of you have heard this said: "A setback is just a setup for a comeback." This may be true, but it also could be an opportunity for Yah to get your attention and to remind you that "you got this" because He has overcome the world.

CONCLUSION

They will know I've been here by the mark I leave.

The journey of following your heart's desire is not an easy one. Stepping out in boldness and wondering if you have truly heard from the Lord is not an easy thing to do. My suggestion to anyone who wishes to make a difference in this world is not to set out on this journey with the wrong motives. Do what you do because it is what you are called by the Most High to do. Do not try to be an influencer. Just be yourself, and you will be an influencer. People gravitate toward authenticity and shy away from phoniness. So often people try to mimic another's journey instead of following their own.

It is important for you to believe that you have found favor in the Father's eyes, and that is why He has a special plan for your life that no one else can carry out but you. We are all favored by Yahweh. He has chosen us all in some way to be world changers, but some just don't know it yet.

I would like to end with this excerpt from *Showing Mary* by Dr. Renita Weems.

So, what does it mean to be favored by God? Does it mean you're different from other women, better than other women, more blessed and chosen than other women? Absolutely not. It means that you have God's undivided attention. You always have had God's attention. But this time you know it in ways you've never known before. You notice now that your plans have become folded and kneaded into God's plan for you. 'You have found favor with God' means that your season to move out and step up to your potential and purpose has arrived. Your plans for yourself have not been tossed out. The favor of God makes them possible, doable, achievable. You are now becoming ready from within. A new self is emerging. You are outgrowing the old ways."

(page 13, emphasis added)

My prayer is that this statement and the other things mentioned in this chapter will resonate with us all and that we will truly realize that Yahweh, the Lord, Elohim, the Creator of the Universe has an awesome plan for us all. He is waiting for us to just step out. So put your foot in the water, and watch the sea open up, for The Lord is saying, "I have plans for you."

REFERENCES

Munroe, Myles (2003). *The Principles and Power of Vision.* Whitaker House

Weems, Renita J. (2002). *Showing Mary.* Warner Books, Inc.

ABOUT THE AUTHOR

Dr. Maxine Collins is devoted to seeing the lives of those around her transformed by renewing their minds in accordance with the Word of God. She is a member of Emmanuel Worship Center in Petersburg, Virginia, serving as minister, Bible teacher, and counselor. Dr. Maxine has a bachelor's degree in business management from the University of Monroe (ULM), a bachelor's in Eastern Biblical Education from Emmanuel Worship Center Bible Institute, a master's in human services/marriage and family counseling from Liberty University, and a ThD in theology from Seraphim Ministries International Bible College. Dr. Maxine has her foundation in the Hebrew roots of her faith, which she has reaped from her studies at Emmanuel Worship Center under the leadership of the late Pastor Joseph P. Green.

She is a lifelong student and has done individual studies for over ten years on the science of the mind and how this science aligns with scripture. With this knowledge, Dr. Maxine developed the 63-Day Mind Challenge Program, which guides the participant through sixty-three days of exercises geared toward transforming destructive thinking patterns, such as doubt, worry, anxiety, and low self-image into healthy, productive thoughts. In response to the studies she has completed, she is working on further developing the program for corporate and business use as well as Biblical.

Dr. Maxine is the director of Advocate Enterprises, a non-profit organization providing scholarship funds for her community's underserved. She also has an instructor and serves on the Seraphim Ministries International Bible College board. Dr. Maxine is the proud mother of one daughter (La'Tesha Collins) and the proud grandmother of four: Isaiah, Jaidah, Daniel, and Nehemiah.

From the Classroom to Beyond

Beyond

RENITA M. COURTNEY

Teaching was never on my radar. Who wants to spend hours a day in a classroom drilling knowledge into kids that aren't theirs? NOT ME! I did everything I thought would lead to a fruitful career in fashion, only to realize that I spent most of the time teaching employees how to execute on the strategies I was hired to enforce. I became a teacher without trying. There is a saying that when we make plans, God laughs. I know He let out a hearty, belly-aching laugh when I quit my job in fashion to return to grad school for a certification in education. But laughing or not, I had no clue just how rewarding the journey would be.

THE JOURNEY BEGINS

The fashion world seemed to be a more exciting career, so I started working in retail as an assistant manager with an enormous amount of responsibilities. While at work one day, I realized that I was doing the very thing I said I wouldn't do. I spent every day as an assistant manager training the cashiers and salespersons about their daily responsibilities. I realized God was showing me that I was doing the very thing I said I would not do. I was teaching—teaching the employees under my supervision every day, instructing them on how to do their jobs, whether they were veterans or new employees.

In the midst of this epiphany, I knew I was using my skills in the wrong profession. This is not where God wanted me to be. I knew what needed to be done. I started praying and asking God for guidance.

In the midst of this career change, I was about to embark upon, the store manager and the district manager offered me the store manager position. It was confusing to be in that situation because they did everything in their power to convince me to take the job. At the same time, I was waiting for confirmation about this change, but deep down I knew what I needed to do. There was a little voice inside of me telling me, *It's time to leave this job.* That voice said, *You need to go back to school and get certified to teach. Let's get started.*

EMBARKING ON A NEW ENDEAVOR

I applied to graduate school and was accepted. I talked to my manager and explained to her why I couldn't take the job offer and turned in my two weeks' notice, leaving a job I thought I was supposed to be in. There was an overwhelming peace that came over me that reassured me that I was definitely making the correct career choices. After this experience, I became more aware of the way events and circumstances are revealed in my life. I talked to my parents about my plans, and they were very supportive, as always.

So I moved from my apartment and made arrangements to move in with them for a year. That's how long it would take for me to get certified. I knew that was going to be an adjustment, especially after living on my own for several years. But I was so excited and ready for this new endeavor. I was willing to do whatever was necessary to accomplish this new goal in my life.

I devoted that year to taking all the classes that were

required to become a certified teacher. I had to study harder than ever because a couple of the classes were difficult, especially the statistics class. I finished all the classes by June. Fortunately, I finished with a GPA higher than a 3.0 and had twenty-nine hours toward a master's degree. At this time, everything was falling in place. God was orchestrating my steps. My advisor was busy looking for somewhere I could do my student teaching. Finally, a position opened up at a girls correctional facility.

I was placed as a child care student-teacher with an exceptional educator. She was patient, very knowledgeable, and was very dedicated to making sure I was going to be the best teacher I could be. After my first week of watching her, I knew this was in God's plan. She demonstrated a genuine relationship with her students, even though they were in a correctional facility. She encouraged the girls to participate in the lessons. She was such a great example of the teacher I wanted to become. I really enjoyed having an opportunity to teach the young ladies. This was an amazing experience.

TEACHING CAREER BEGINS

In the meantime, I was applying for various teaching positions. I was offered one in July. I was so excited. I accepted it and started my first teaching job in August. This was the beginning of a thirty-two-year career as a high school educator. When I first started teaching, needless to say, I was young and had a lot to learn about life and people. This was definitely orchestrated by God, because when I was in college, my mind was not to become an educator.

My journey as an influencer started with this position. My first teaching position was both rewarding and challenging. I learned the importance of developing relationships with students, and I immediately fell in love with teaching. After nine years in my first position, I accepted another teaching position closer to home.

My philosophy of teaching during my career was: *to be a successful teacher, I had to be dedicated.* I needed to maintain a positive attitude and love educating children. It was an amazing career that required a lot of preparation time in order to have the best presentation for the daily lessons I'd prepared for my students. I always felt that students needed to know why you are teaching. Oftentimes I would end up telling my students that I knew I was supposed to be there for them. I loved what I was doing and wanted to make sure they were learning all they could. It was so rewarding knowing I had imparted valuable lessons and knowledge in them—lessons that will help them become contributing citizens of society.

The next teaching position I accepted was definitely a great example of how God had orchestrated my life even when I wasn't quite sure how everything was going to turn out. It wasn't apparent until I was in the midst of the situation. I was thinking about applying for jobs closer to home, so I started looking for school systems. One day, one of my former students came to school to visit me. She had graduated from Longwood University.

While we were talking, she mentioned she was applying for teaching positions at several school systems in the area. She had an application from a school system that she really wasn't interested in at the time. She asked me if I wanted it, and of course I said yes since it was closer to my home. I immediately applied for the family and consumer science teaching position and was called the next day for an interview. This was an exciting time in my life. I realized God had his hand on my life and was ordering my steps. I prayed about the position and trusted God totally because I knew He made this opportunity available for me. I went to the interview, sat down, and answered every question with great ease and confidence. Before the interview was over, they offered me the position. All I could do was thank God because He definitely orchestrated this entire situation. After I was hired, I found out the teacher retiring had also taught me in high school.

I started my new teaching position in August 1981. My first week of new teacher training was amazing. I knew I was walking in my purpose. This is what I was born to do. I was so excited with the new position and new environment. After the training, I felt like I could handle any situation that would come up, but guess what? To my surprise, everything did not go as I expected.

After teaching several years, I was given a class of eighth and ninth graders who made me question my teaching career. I did not feel like an influencer at all. That class challenged me more than I'd ever experienced. Imagine having wonderful experiences all day, and this class comes in, and you feel like they're terrorizing you. At this time, I was given advice from several veteran teachers. I decided to do some research on how to handle behavior problems. After talking to my colleagues, I tried to incorporate some of their advice with that class. The first thing they told me was to figure out what was going on in the life of the students that may be causing the disruptive behavior in the class—try to establish a relationship with the students, talk to the students, and let them know I cared about them and their educational experience.

Another veteran teacher told me not to let them upset me but to remain calm in the situation. Most of the time the students were just looking for attention they may not be receiving at home or from family. It was very important to remain calm when the behavior occurred. I was told to document every time the behavior happened, contact my administrator, have a parent conference if necessary, and have a meeting that included everyone associated with the student.

One of my colleagues suggested coming up with a behavior plan including strategies that could improve the student's behavior. After the plan was completed, I was to discuss it with the student, the parent, and the principal. This was definitely an opportunity to be an efficacious influencer.

The majority of my teaching experience was phenomenal and very rewarding. So much so if given an opportunity, I would do it all over again. I loved my job and my students, spending time with them and getting to know them.

MAKING A DIFFERENCE

There were many days when I bought breakfast and lunch for students. I washed clothes on several occasions. I opened my home several times. My total teaching experience would not have been complete without establishing relationships with the students. Sponsoring a school club and becoming the dance team and the step team coach for several years helped elevate my position as an influencer. The club was a part of the curriculum I was teaching, so it was included in the daily lesson plans. I became the coach of the dance team after several students approached me and asked if I would be the sponsor.

I didn't say yes at first. After thinking about the impact, it would have on the students who participated on the team, I said yes. Coaching the dance and step team was very rewarding. The students who participated learned valuable leadership skills that would help them throughout their life. All the organizations voted for their officers/leaders. They learned to respect each other, to listen to each other, work together, participate as a group in competitions, plan, and organize meetings or performances. This was a crucial position since I was definitely influencing their way of thinking in many areas. The dance team loved performing for the student body and participating in competitions.

The step team was a similar endeavor. Eventually, I realized how time consuming it was with the rehearsals after school and the performances at the basketball games. By this time, my youngest daughter was attending the school. The step team practices were interfering with my daughter's time at home to relax, eat dinner, and focus on her homework. Since I'd become a mother, I was determined and dedicated to be the best I could be to my daughters, so that meant some changes had to be made. So I stopped coaching the step team in order to allow my daughter an opportunity to enjoy our mother-daughter relationship. I felt I had to give my daughter the attention and time she deserved.

LIVING LIFE AS AN EXAMPLE

As a teacher and role model, it was so important that I lived my life as an example for my students. I will admit I may not have realized the importance of the position as much at the beginning of my career, but it didn't take long for me to realize that my students were watching everything I said as well as my every move. It was just like being a parent and your children emulate your behavior and everything you say. Anyone who is a role model or influencer is setting examples, whether you intend to or not.

Whether you're an educator, supervisor, doctor, lawyer, salesperson, administrator, or a political leader, we all have a responsibility to set an example. We must always consider our role in others' lives and how we may impact them. Children—young people—are so impressionable. We have to oversee their television shows, music, and books. As a mother, I made sure my daughters watched TV shows that would stimulate learning and were fun-filled and entertaining. I monitored the music they listened to and tried to monitor the books they read. They both were avid readers, and I promised them when they finished a book, I would take them to the library to get a new one or buy a new one.

When I was teaching the lessons on parenting and child development, there were lessons on cognitive development in children. I stressed to my students the importance of them being role models. You must be proactive in your children's development and education. Allowing myself to be a positive influence on my students every day definitely was an amazing blessing.

INFLUENCING BEYOND THE CLASSROOM

When I think about my influence beyond the classroom, I remember inviting my fashion students to begin a new project. In order to participate, they would need to stay after school. Once I informed them about what they would be doing, they were really excited to learn how to knit. They made a scarf for themselves, and we made scarves for the Salvation Army or a shelter—basically, people in need. The students were so excited about this project that they stayed after school and worked really hard, especially when we talked about how this could help a person or family. We worked together; the students helped each other with their scarves. Overall, the most rewarding moment surrounding this endeavor was when we delivered the scarves. The thank yous and smiles from the people who received our donations made them feel so elated, so much so that this was a continuous project for many years with my students.

After teaching my students how to knit, I spent twenty-plus years knitting various projects and giving them away, not knowing this would lead to me being asked to be in charge of The Prayer Shawl Ministry at my church. I knew when I was asked, that this was my life coming full circle. The ministry is a group of ladies who crochet and knit items for people in need. This has made me an influencer that I never thought I would be. The ministry donates hats and scarves to various elementary schools and shelters, as well as throws and lap blankets to various nursing homes, cancer centers, and kidney dialysis centers.

On a trip to Ghana, West Africa, with the Uniquely Chosen Ministry, under the direction of my first lady, we were fortunate enough to send baby blankets, shawls, and two hundred-plus washcloths to the children at an elementary school. Everyone who received a donation from us was so appreciative. That was an experience I will cherish for the rest of my life.

Being a Girl Scout leader for approximately eleven years also afforded me a chance to influence young ladies. I spent time with them once a month teaching the valuable lessons that were already established by the Girl Scout headquarters. These lessons were created to encourage learning and participation. The young ladies earned badges that boosted their confidence with every one received. This experience was rewarding for the girls as well as the parents.

I also taught a Sunday school class at my church for several years, which was very enriching. I spent a lot of time praying and studying God's Word to prepare for the lessons. I realized I would be imparting significant and life-changing information from the Bible that would reshape the lives of these young people forever, making it even more monumental. Expounding on the Word of God was a phenomenal learning adventure. Not only did it entail teaching, but it necessitated being an example to all of them. This position changed my life forever when I realized the enormous influence I would have on the students in the class.

BEING A GOOD LISTENER

It wasn't until I was in my thirties that I realized I had been given the gift of listening. I didn't know how impactful this gift could be. One day I was thinking about my life in my early thirties and realized some of my friends would call me to discuss their life problems or concerns, expecting a positive response or solution from me. I would always listen and give them the best solution to whatever they were dealing with.

At first, if I can be honest, it was challenging because I too had a few life issues that I needed help with from time to time. But I realized early on that this was a special position God had placed me in. Listening and basically being a confidant became a phenomenal experience. Knowing that my friends trusted me to help to come up with solutions for their concerns was an honor, and I did not take it lightly.

IMPACTING THE WORLD AS AN INFLUENCER

Merriam-Webster defines an influencer as a person who inspires or guides the actions of others. When I think about other female influencers or persons who inspire, I think about people like former First Lady Michelle Obama, TV personalities such as Oprah Winfrey, prominent minister's wives, doctors, lawyers, educators on all levels and people in various other occupations. People tend to follow or listen to these people based on their status or how they feel they can benefit from being associated with them. Influencers often don't realize how they impact people and society. In most situations, we are under a microscope every day, so we have to decide how we want to transform the people in our sector.

Being an influencer has really changed every aspect of my life. Even when I didn't realize I was in that position, I was impacting the lives of many. God puts us in places and situations for a reason. He already knows the plans He has for us and orchestrates our life from birth. It's up to us to stay on course. We must understand our purpose and walk in it.

ABOUT THE AUTHOR

Destined to change lives, Renita M. Courtney is a woman with a heart for God and for people. With more than fifty years of service, thirty-two years of teaching, twenty years of leadership serving church and community, she has embodied a spirit of philanthropy since she was a young girl.

After earning her degree from the illustrious Virginia State University in home economics and business, she began her career as a teacher and businesswoman. Everything her hands touched turned to gold. She used her resources to pour into the lives of her students and family.

Highly decorated with awards after her time in the classroom, Renita retired and pursued a second career giving of her time and efforts in ministry. She served as the leader of the Mount Olivet Prayer Shawl ministry while traveling for missionary work in Ghana, West Africa. She has continued to create spaces for women to connect over the opportunity to share in their creativity and purpose. She enjoys spending time with her husband, two daughters, and grandson.

Wisdom and Light

TARA D. HENRY

Light itself has no sound, but it can be heard. There is a phenomenon called sonoluminescence, which turns sound into light. It occurs when high-frequency sound vibrates tiny gas bubbles to reach star-like temperatures and emit flashes or sparks of light; a spark ignites a flame, which can be seen. You are probably asking yourself, what does this have to do with wisdom and light? Everything! As we navigate through life, our light, which is energy, speaks. It alerts those around us of our attitude and mood without us having to say a word. In retrospect, light can be heard through the words that are spoken out of the mouth. *For the mouth speaks from the overflow of the heart* (Matthew 12:34b NKJV). It is a silent power that starts from within, in turn, being heard from without.

In the Holy Scripture, light is a powerful symbol of Elohim's presence and knowledge. In the book of Genesis, the first thing God creates is light, separating it from the darkness. This light is a physical representation of God's divine wisdom, which guides us through life and illuminates our path. Light is often used as a metaphor for knowledge and wisdom. In John 8:12, Yeshua says, *"I am the light of the world. Whoever follows me will never walk in darkness but will have the light of life."* Light is also seen as a symbol of the presence of God as we live a life in accordance to His will and being a positive influence on those around us. By letting our light shine and reflecting the light of the Messiah in our lives, we can bring hope, inspiration, and guidance to those who need it.

"Follow the North Star." It is what our ancestors used to say when they were trying to find freedom during a time that was horrendous for them. Since the North Star does not move with the rotation of the Earth, it is a fixed star. It was important for them to find that particular star. Once they found the North Star, which is the biggest and brightest star in the sky, they knew that they were headed in the right direction; hope was stirred up. A star was also the guiding light that the wise men followed to the birthplace of the Messiah. In both instances, stars can be seen as symbols of guidance and direction. What exactly is a star? It is a ball filled with so much energy that it cannot help but shine. Have you ever been outside at night when the moon is new and looked up in that dark sky and saw twinkling stars? Well, those stars are energy, shining in the darkness. When you are the light, it is your opportunity to shine in the darkness so that those who are looking up can see.

I read a quote one day that said, "Your energy introduces you before you speak." How simple yet profound is that? One day at work, I had a conversation with a former principal from the school where I teach, and she informed me that she had interviewed a former student for a substitute teacher position. During the interview, she had asked the student about teachers who had influenced her to want to serve as a substitute teacher, and she mentioned my name. I was surprised by that because I had never taught that student nor had any real interaction with her. From time to time, I would see her in the hallways and just say hello or smile at her. She was one of those young ladies who always had a negative disposition or mean look, so a lot of school staff did not interact positively with her. As a result, to hear that she named me as someone she looked up to was surprising. However, it confirmed that our energy, our light, shines in places and catches the eyes of others without us realizing it. It is so important for us to walk in the light and to be connected to the light source to give someone else hope, regardless of how they look and no matter whether you know them or not. You are a light; your energy will have an impact on them.

In the Bible, the concept of light is often used to represent spiritual illumination, truth, and righteousness. Similarly, the light of a person can refer to their character, behavior, and influence on those around them. The Bible also frequently uses the metaphor of "light" to refer to the spiritual influence and impact that a person can have on others. In Matthew 5:14-16 NKJV, Yeshua teaches, *"You are the light of the world. A town built on a hill cannot be hidden. Neither do people light a lamp and put it under a bowl. Instead, they put it on its stand, and it gives light to everyone in the house. In the same way, let your light shine before others, that they may see your good deeds and glorify your Father in heaven."*

This passage emphasizes the importance of being a positive influence on others through our actions, behavior, and words. When we live according to God's will and exhibit traits like kindness, compassion, and integrity, it can inspire others to do the same and bring glory to God. By living a life of faith and obedience to God, we can impact others in a positive way and point them toward a life of hope and truth. The light of a person can also bring comfort, hope, and encouragement to those who are struggling in darkness. Additionally, Ephesians 5:8 NKJV says, *"For you were once darkness, but now you are light in the Lord. Walk as children of light."* This verse highlights that we have been transformed by the light of Messiah and are called to live in a way that reflects this transformation.

By living as "children of light," we can impact others with the love and grace of God, drawing them closer to him. In addition, Paul speaks about the impact of the light of Messiah on our lives in 2 Corinthians 4:6 NKJV, saying, *"For God, who said, 'Let light shine out of darkness,' made his light shine in our hearts to give us the light of the knowledge of God's glory displayed in the face of Messiah."* This verse highlights the transformative power of the light of Messiah, which can bring spiritual enlightenment and understanding to those who seek it.

WHAT GOES ON INTERNALLY MANIFESTS EXTERNALLY

What about when you do not feel like a light is within you? Is it possible to always have a light within, especially when your heart is broken? How do we move? I found myself in a situation where my heart was truly broken and my feelings deeply hurt by someone that I truly loved, and it had me to a point where I did not think I could finish this chapter. How could I possibly write about light and wisdom when I was hurting? At that time, I did not feel like I had it in me; I did not feel encouraged, so I did not feel like I could encourage anyone else.

Unbeknownst to me, my energy was being felt by others, regardless of if I was in their presence or over the phone, even though I was trying to hide the inner turmoil that I was feeling. That is how powerful light/energy is. If our light is dim or hidden, it may not have as much of an impact on others. In Matthew 5:15 NKJV, Yeshua warns against hiding one's light, saying, *"Neither do people light a lamp and put it under a bowl. Instead, they put it on its stand, and it gives light to everyone in the house."* This means that we should not be afraid to let our light shine under any difficult or uncomfortable circumstances.

Fortunately, because I am connected to the source of the light, I was able to continue writing. I am not sure how many of you all have a spiritual relationship with God, or even if you believe in Him, but it is because of Him and the wisdom that He has given me that I am able to go on and continue to walk in his light so that my light can still shine, regardless of my disappointment. *"For you yourself light my lamp; Yahuah my Elohim makes my darkness light"* (Psalm 18:28 *The Scriptures*). This is important because Yahuah helps us to navigate through darkness. In dark places and times, we need Him.

Light has long been associated with knowledge and understanding, and for good reason. The light of the sun enables us to see the world around us and gain knowledge about our surroundings. In the same way, the light of wisdom illuminates our minds and allows us to gain knowledge and understanding of the spirit within us. Light is so dope that its various colors have therapeutic benefits. For example, according to some experts, when we are exposed to blue light during the day, we may feel more alert, focused, and productive.

Light gives us strength, it energizes us, and brings us joy. Think about when you go outside on a sunny day, as compared to a cloudy or rainy day; how does it make you feel? For me, when it's sunny outside, I have so much energy that I am able to accomplish many tasks. Anything that is bright, I tend to be drawn to it. I am talking about things, such as sunlight; the moonlight, especially when it is full; and the stars in the sky at night.

To look up at that dark sky and see those stars twinkling just does something to me, and I become awestruck. That is the way people look at those who have that light within them. Did you not know that light gives us transformational power? Well, it does. Think about it: The light that is within us is so powerful that it can change someone else's demeanor and possibly someone's outlook on life, specifically their lives. A person could observe you for a while wondering what is it about this person that makes them the way that they are. Their curiosity is going to draw them toward you, which could give you an opportunity to share with them where your light comes from.

Like light, wisdom is a gift from God that enables us to see and understand the world around us. It allows us to discern right from wrong, make good decisions, and live in harmony with others. In the Bible, wisdom and light are often used to represent spiritual truths and guidance from God. Wisdom is generally understood to refer to the ability to make sound judgments and decisions based on knowledge and experience and to live in accordance with God's will.

Proverbs 9:10 NKJV says, *"The fear of the Lord is the beginning of wisdom, and knowledge of the Holy One is understanding."* This means that true wisdom begins with a reverence for God and an acknowledgement of his sovereignty over all things. In addition, James 1:5 NKJV says, *"If any of you lacks wisdom, let him ask of God, who gives to all liberally and without reproach, and it will be given to him."* This verse encourages believers to seek wisdom from God through prayer and meditation on His Word. As the psalmist writes, *"The fear of the Lord is the beginning of wisdom; all who follow his precepts have good understanding"* (Psalm 111:10 KJV).

Wisdom also enables us to recognize our own limitations and to seek guidance and support from God. Ultimately, wisdom is a spiritual quality that is intimately connected to our relationship with God. As we seek to grow in wisdom, we draw closer to God and deepen our understanding of His divine plan for our lives. As we walk in the light of His wisdom, we can be a beacon of hope and guidance to others, illuminating the way to a brighter and more fulfilling future.

Our light influences our atmosphere as well as those around us. However, we need wisdom to strengthen our light. Wisdom is often described as the ability to make good judgments and decisions based on knowledge and experience. It is a quality that is highly valued in many cultures and is often associated with the aged, as they have had more time to accumulate knowledge and experience. However, wisdom is not limited to the elderly; anyone can cultivate wisdom through a combination of learning, application, reflection, and experience. To cultivate wisdom, we must first know its attributes.

According to James 3:17 KJV, wisdom is pure, meaning it is peaceable, gentle, and easy to be entreated, full of mercy and good fruits, without partiality, without hypocrisy—not phony.

From my personal experience, wisdom is not forceful. It is concerned with our well-being, it is patient, fruit bearing, and sincere. As a teacher, I have not only observed how students react to some teachers, but I have also heard them mention that they don't like certain teachers because they are fake. They try to behave as if they like them, but they can tell that it is not genuine. They can smile, laugh with them, and pat them on the back, but the students feel their true energy.

Walking in wisdom is not as hard as we have been made to believe; it is basically applying our past experiences to making functional decisions. Can I influence someone in a positive way if I live a dysfunctional lifestyle? Absolutely not! Whereas we all have the power to influence others, it is wisdom that helps us to decide if the influence will be positive or negative.

Light is often used in the Bible to represent truth, righteousness, and God's presence. John 8:12 NKJV says, *"I am the light of the world. He who follows Me shall not walk in darkness, but have the light of life."* This verse emphasizes Yeshua is the ultimate source of spiritual light and that those who follow Him will be guided by His truth and righteousness.

Similarly, Psalm 119:105 NKJV says, *"Your word is a lamp for my feet, and a light to my path."* This verse highlights the importance of studying and meditating on God's Word to receive spiritual guidance and direction.

The energy of a person can have a significant impact on others, both positively and negatively. The energy of a person refers to their overall mood, emotions, and vibe, which can be felt by others in their presence. When a person has positive energy, they tend to radiate warmth, happiness, and confidence. This can make others feel comfortable, happy, and relaxed in their presence. Positive energy can also be contagious, spreading to those around us and uplifting their moods.

If any of you are teachers, have ever been a classroom teacher, or just simply observed people in a learning environment where there may have been one or more people not engaged, it could have been due to the energy of the teacher or instructor. I have had conversations with coworkers who have taught some of the same students as I have. They would tell me, "So and so just sits in their seat and stares at me. They are never engaged with what we are doing." While, they are fully engaged and interacting with me and their peers in my class.

On the other hand, when a person has negative energy, it can bring down the mood and emotions of those around them. Negative energy can manifest as anger, sadness, anxiety, or frustration, and it can create tension and discomfort in social situations. Negative energy can also be contagious, spreading to others and causing them to feel uneasy or distressed. Overall, a person's energy can impact others in a variety of ways, and it is important to be aware of the energy we bring into social situations. By cultivating positive energy and regulating our emotions, we can have a positive impact on those around us and create a more harmonious and supportive environment.

Wisdom and light are both important spiritual concepts that represent God's guidance, truth, and presence in our lives. Seeking wisdom through prayer and meditation on God's Word and following the light of Messiah are essential for living a righteous and fulfilling life according to Biblical teachings. Light it seems has been a theme, message, and moral take-away in my life. The message of wisdom and light is—even during times of heartache, despair, disappointment, and/or loneliness —the Light is always there, waiting for us to reconnect and recharge. It is our power source, driving and urging us to shine because, like it or not, we were put here to be a light for those in darkness.

So, when people tend to be drawn to you— they want to talk to you, ask you questions, or be near you— don't think that it is strange. In some instances, a person may not say anything to you, and you do not find out until years later that you have influenced them. It is because of the wisdom that you walk in and the light that is within you. As we walk in the light of God's wisdom, we can be a beacon of hope and guidance to others, illuminating the way to a brighter and more fulfilling future. We are called to be lights, a walking safe haven to those walking in darkness. Don't worry about being an eye catcher. Be someone who enlightens. Beauty and light both come from within, so today, consider if what you are feeding yourself is going to bring forth light or darkness. Beauty without light is vain. Selah. Think about that.

Most importantly, do not take lightly the power that you have to influence others. It is a gift, therefore keep yourself nurtured with positive thoughts and people. Use wisdom by keeping yourself connected to the source of wisdom and living in the light that He has given you.

Shalom.

ABOUT THE AUTHOR

Tara Henry grew up in Suitland, Maryland, and Manassas, Virginia, and currently resides in Central Virginia. She is the mother of one son, Luzard Christopher Henry, who is her personal gift from the Most High. As the owner and operator of Fourth Tribe LLC, an apparel company with a royal flare, Tara can show off her love for creative fashion. She has been a public educator for eighteen years, working with students in both special and general education. She does not look at the young people that she teaches as mere students, she sees them as her children.

Tara has a bachelor of arts in political science, an M.Ed. in special education, and an Ed.S. in educational leadership, and she is currently studying the Hebrew language and culture. Tara's passion is to challenge others to think beyond the external and realize that we must nurture our internal and spiritual being as we live from the inside out.

Black Women Control the Narrative by Writing the Real Black Story

DR. YVONNE SMITH-JONES

My people, Africans brought to the shores of Fort Comfort, now Fort Monroe, Virginia, and later, some historians said, Jamestown, Virginia. Stories from our ancestors referred to a small rural community in Charles City, Virginia, as Little Jamestown.

Understanding the Origin and Foundation: A Black Child Is Born

Life could have started for me on the same land and shores as my native heritage. My ancestors were slaves, shackled in chains, packed like sardines in ships and boats, and left to survive the journey with little to no attention given to their needs.

They were selected because of having healthy bodies, exhibiting acute abilities to learn, and modeling impeccable survival skills to see another day. Hard work and focusing on many tasks were mechanisms to keep minds clear in order to avoid brutal beatings and killings. The Europeans thought they were getting cheap labor, but they underestimated the potential of these Africans. They had well-developed brains as well as healthy bodies. They had metacognition skills with the ability to think critically and reason. Meanwhile, the Europeans concentrated on building their wealth and ignored the obvious: These slaves were thinkers.

In Virginia, the Chesapeake Bay was the main waterway for most Africans. The river and land were the environments that they had to navigate. They survived by using these environments to live in this new world, being thankful for their African rituals and remembering their loved ones from whom they departed and the act of valuing blessings was institutionalized.

Why do African Americans place such an emphasis and value on education? The owners restricted the slaves from their routine behavior and movement and prohibited them from learning to read and write. As they observed, they saw books as tools to access the language to communicate more clearly. Early on, slaves realized that education was the golden seed to plant and sow a better tomorrow. At this point, the African-American culture was born from the act of enslavement. While connecting the points of light and hope, they became rumbustious and rebellious.

These restricted behaviors unveiled love in many languages through chats, drums, and songs. Slaves embraced the act of marriage and having families. This knowledge disclosed a story of a blessed people moving from slavery to brilliance. Amplifying voices to convey messages from our ancestors left a legacy of undefined richness, which exposes itself when injustices occur to deflate the positive momentum of African Americans. This undefined richness is our Black cultural trait. The coordinates on this map operationally defined Black culture as:

- exhibiting hard work, grit, and grind.
- seeking the power of education.
- navigating the environment.
- using rebellion to fight for rights.
- applying mental therapy of chats, songs, and nonverbal cues to communicate.

- embracing marriage and family.
- valuing being thankful for many blessings (Smith-Jones, 2019).

These attributes are at the core of our existence. Get acquainted with these traits because, in the midst of pine trees and corn and wheat fields, Black babies are being born with a spirit of hope and joy. In one rural household, a bundle of joy coming to life with a loud cry indicating arrival into a world of uncharted waters shows a healthy Black child is born. And life started with one hundred percent dependency on its caregivers. This dependent stage of development required caring for basic needs, developing the senses, providing a nurturing environment, and directing the compass to point the path to an unknown story. A map began to develop, but there were no pictorial cues or representations to guide the direction.

At this point, it was a world without words as a form of communication. Sounds had no meaning and walking was not a mode of movement. God knew the coordinates to reveal harmony and foster relationships. Although one cannot fathom the inscrutable mind of God, the map of one's destiny is plotted with coordinates displaying the longitude and latitude of each ordered pair in our lives. As the baby grew, reaching the independent stage of development, the world opened as a flower.

Making sense, understanding the environment, and seeing the beauty of it all ushered in the autonomous stage of life. The story started with God's faith, hope, and love in making the journey to unknown shores. Let's dissect the need and power of the village effect in defining Black culture.

KNOWING AND USING THE VILLAGE

The home was the first learning institution, church, community, and then school. Having independence when growing up meant making so many decisions while experiencing successes and failures. Indoctrinated lessons learned in the home and church were the origin of understanding right from wrong. Self-discipline was the order of the day. Church was a place where salvation was nurtured, Biblical stories made the Bible meaningful, and Bible verses were read and memorized. Church folks served as one's second family.

When living with two sisters and one brother, sharing, being respectful, displaying good manners, and socializing with relatives and friends were ways to develop one's social and emotional development. The desire and love for school were so visible. Having dark brown skin and nappy hair were never areas of concentration. Meanwhile, God has granted me many talents, a wealth of knowledge, and tools to control the course of an unknown journey. During elementary school, I attended an all-Black school, but starting in the seventh grade, my classmates were natives, Black students plus a few Caucasians.

Teachers introduced me to literature, fiction, and nonfiction books. My areas of interest were always mathematics and science. Learning was cool, but I was not a bookworm or a nerd. School was fun, and I found opportunities to engage in exciting activities. Playing school and admiring teachers were mental models for a career in teaching. While my siblings were all basketball players in high school, I was the co-captain of the cheering squad. Participating in varied and challenging activities were means that drove and motivated me. Getting connected with others and understanding differences were the central tenets of belongingness.

My mother was the community carpool mom, and neighbors always watched out for the children. Our home had an open-door policy for the community. The people in this community were always ready to give love, food, and comfort to one another. Although education attainment and job levels were at the low end of the job hierarchy, people were happy. *Poverty* was never a word used in the community. My father worked for the federal government, and my mother was a housekeeper until I went to school, then she was a home healthcare assistant working and caring for white families.

My mother was given albums of classical music, and at an early age, a love and desire for classical music emerged. Tchaikovsky's "Fifth Symphony," "Swan Lake," and "The Nutcracker" quieted the beating heart and slowed the racing brain. Our family had the basics plus more. As a family, once a month, we took mini trips to different cities and counties in Virginia. We had vacations and stayed with relatives in different states during the summer. Many aunts were school teachers, and my uncles attended the military along with my father.

I was voted student government president for the high school and served in many events. People knew me, but I would not say that I was popular. I loved to laugh, joke, and party. Being around people was awesome. Entering boy-craving mode and falling in and out of puppy love was ongoing. Learning from all types of people grew my neurons and dendrites. Having fun, going to church or loving school were not distractors toward my career aspiration.

In 1975, I graduated in the top ten of the one hundred and twenty-five graduates in my rural school. That year, we won the state championship in football, and I attended Girls State to learn about local and state government. There was no doubt when graduating from high school regarding career paths. I was accepted to a variety of schools in and out of state, however, a small historically black university in Norfolk, Virginia, drew me in like a magnet. I organized my financial aid, grants, and scholarship opportunities. School officials were motivational and helpful if needed. By navigating and learning about college life, I was ready. My sister attended college before me, so I knew what to anticipate.

Diversity, equity, and inclusiveness had not directly impacted my life at this stage of the game. This decade in my life was living out the dream of integration. While living in this small rural community in Virginia where eighty-five percent of the population was Black, one had a feeling of conquering the world and becoming successful. Positive thinking and being ambitious were hidden, silent attributes of my personality. Being young and exhibiting growing pains, a person did not always pay attention to the seriousness of life. Upon touring the university's campus, the student union building was where I found a place to worship each Sunday morning.

College was terrific, a time to meet new people and try things. For four years, young people and professionals extended the village with support and nurturing. Making friends, building relationships, and trusting others were essential in understanding college life. I cheered at four basketball games for the university, was vice president of the Student Virginia Educational Association, honor student, and Phi Delta Kappa member, but Greek sororities were not sought.

The need to create a sisterhood bond was not a missing element in my life at that time. Always valuing the sisterhood of sororities as another component in expanding a sense of community and village living. Focusing on my studies, enjoying student teaching, and giving service and time to others allowed the rays of the light to grow brighter. Let's be real, hardships, restless nights, worrying about extra money, and making good grades were embedded into me throughout this journey of becoming. Reality kept me concentrating on the here-and-now domain of life.

Tips to guide your thinking, staying on the course, and making it to the finish line:

- Have faith and connect with family.
- Give back and visit your community.
- Make contributions to those in need.
- Volunteer and care for others.
- Avoid toxic people.

- Lift as you climb.
- Be the authentic you.
- Avoid being arrogant—be humble.
- Pursue excellence.

Determination and inner strength were sometimes visible or non-visible. Doors were open, but there were door stops to impede entrance into other well-established villages. Discomfort raised its ugly head when living in a village-like atmosphere. Silos and isolation were unavoidable. Issues of social justice and having critical conversations were segments of learning and understanding while not fearing to ask questions and clarify explanations. Many obstacles, barriers, and challenges hacked the pathway while living in one's social, emotional, and cultural turfs. The journey was not easy, and missteps in the path caused setbacks and challenges, but forging onward to the desired career path of teaching was never a dream deferred.

USING THE TABLE EFFECT AND MAKING FOOTPRINTS

Finally, the big day of graduation arrived with joy, happiness, and family celebrating this extraordinary achievement in life. Actually, the ticket to guide the journey into the wonderful world of work had arrived. It was my license as a certified middle school teacher. The reality of the dream unfolded with a classroom full of real students with many different challenges. Game on, it was my opportunity to grow, develop, and give back to students. The challenges were taken on as goals, and the determination to fulfill them was crafted. Being in a teaching and learning environment, the need to pull the strength of the village emerged like a bright light shining on injustices inside and outside of a place called school. It was time to learn and apply new knowledge.

While living so close to Williamsburg, Virginia, I often wondered why so many workers at the second oldest institution of higher learning in America were Black, but the students were Caucasians. I set a goal to get accepted and attain a master's degree from this college. Upon attaining that master's degree, the silent voice began to rise up and amplify with a burning need to defend students and educators. Acquiring memberships and leading many professional and volunteer organizations impeded on my social life, but I got married and brought my husband along on a bumpy road to instill a sense of self-worth into the lives of these wonderful children. As a Black woman, living behind the scene was normal, however speaking engagements from churches, civic organizations, and educational arenas dominated my free time. A blessing was showered upon me at the age of twenty-nine to become a principal and lead a school. Understanding, establishing, and implementing school policies and procedures were at the heart of being successful in this venue.

It was during this time my lenses were laser-focused on external issues impeding the process of teaching and learning. Parents and the community became vocal participants in expressing issues or complimenting the direction of the school.

Learning and calling on the village to support me in obtaining a doctorate in educational administration dominated my thinking. Knowledge is power, and education is a means to an end. Always include God and education in the formula to arrive at success. Opportunities to teach graduate-level courses were extended by the University of Virginia, Virginia Commonwealth University, Regent University, Virginia State University, and the College of William and Mary. These environments were assisting me in charting the course in diverse territories. Being exposed to many unique and different people assisted me in understanding how people think, express opinions, and address others in ways not respecting the rights of human beings.

Tangible action moves authentic conversations to the table, on the menu, in the chairs, or as a centerpiece. Words frame the conversations, but action drives the change. The table effect was shouted from the voice of Congresswoman Shirley Chisholm in 1970: "If they don't give you a seat at the table, bring a folding table." President Barack Obama stated, "Don't just get involved. Fight for your seat at the table. Better yet, fight for a seat at the head of the table." Former First Lady Eleanor Roosevelt echoed, "Great minds discuss ideas, average minds discuss events, and small minds discuss people." Senator Elizabeth Warren added, "If you don't have a seat at the table, you're probably on the menu." Educator Yvonne Smith-Jones stated, "Direct energies toward changing the dynamics of the member of the table, putting policy on the table, and using the table as a platform to bring about change."

The goal is for more Black women to cover the table with a cloth of fulfillment, to place the mats on the table to protect and safeguard from injustices, to negotiate at the table, to break bread at the table, to eat the fruit of equity at the table, and to avoid being a guy on the side—aim for the head seat at the table.

THE TABLE EFFECT: MOVING CHAOS TO CHANGE

If you want differences, then you need to see the differences and concentrate on needed changes. While working at the central office level, policy was the main vehicle to change. As a leader, one is afforded the opportunities to change teaching resources, materials, teachers, teaching strategies, and the list goes on and on. Change is gradual and needs to be planned. Sometimes the leader operated at a crowded or a tilted table trying to resolve vexing issues. It seemed that leveraging change was the construct, idea, or policy driving my mission of teaching and learning. Next, I joined local and state boards. Then, it was explicit the map was revealing the path of a servant leader.

As a servant leader, I allowed myself to engage in courageous conversations, work with people and students in marginalized communities, and forged opportunities to have conversations to learn about other people. Traveling in states and other countries provided a coherent vision. The vision provided simpler and more perspicuous explanations of my calling. The vision was 20/20 lucid. Believe beyond what you can see. Build bridges, live beyond yourself, and laugh and smile about our struggles.

The KEY is to keep educating yourself (**K**eep patience, **E**ducate the mind, and be **Y**ou). Today while working as an impact coach, leaders soliciting coaches are seeking ways to remove the noise from their minds to foster clarity. Clarity is needed to unwind and unleash. As leaders dump their brains to avoid strain, many find clarity and proceed toward logical meaning in many situations. At the end of the day, seek happiness.

A single person cannot lead change but can cast a broader net to obtain a range of individuals. There is no right or wrong way to lead, however, bringing and leveraging the collective gifts of staff merged ideas and decision-making. Allow one's moral compass to frame self-reflections and conversations triggering ideas when problem-solving. Make no mistakes, if you lead with others, value their contributions.

Takeaways from Leaving Footprints:

- Employ forward, out-of-the-box thinking to tap into intrinsic desires.
- Aim to forge strong partnerships with the people.
- Transform workspace to hubs of learning cubicles.
- Guide colleagues to become strategic thinkers utilizing a time for self-reflection.
- Organize and rearrange routines and practices.

- Employ new positive practices connected to old negative practices.
- Dismantle existing structures and practices with no value added.

THE IMPACT OF A BLACK WOMAN

When I need to talk, the **Black Woman**
  has an ear.
When I need time to recharge, the **Black
  Woman** is ever ready.
When I feel useless, the **Black Woman**
  directs meaning.
When stress takes over, the **Black
  Woman** is the only shining light.
When I feel clueless, the **Black Woman**
  prompts the thinking.
When I feel weak, the **Black Woman**
  provides strength.
When I need to organize, the **Black
  Woman** orders the mess.
When I need to listen, the **Black Woman**
  starts the conversation.

We are not lost as a people. We are complicated and need time to get acquainted with ourselves, then deal with the challenges of living and understanding others. Think about a history deriving from so many unknowns, being captured in a capsule of enslavement, and jumping on demand to obey and serve. The world sees the outer core of us and makes many assumptions. We live the true self every day. Learn to love yourself and one another, keep life simple, but have dreams, goals, and aspirations. Rely on the map, being guided by the Lord. He will direct your path. Remember that the impact of a woman, especially a Black woman, is powerful. One can be sassy and classy.

Every educator needs a village. The rural, urban, or suburban girl can create a map and chart the course of self-fulfillment. This opportunity is given to all. Seek living, keep learning, and the path to leadership will emerge. Establish a relationship with a woman, and she will tell you her narrative, and you will see endless potential. Believe in us.

ABOUT THE AUTHOR

Dr. Yvonne Smith-Jones currently works full-time and part-time as an impact coach collaborating with many school-based administrators in the Commonwealth of Virginia for a School-University Research Network in the School of Education at the College of William and Mary. She served as the director of the Project ALL leadership project in the educational leadership department at Virginia Commonwealth University from 2009 to 2011. She retired in 2009 after working for thirty-one years as a teacher, principal and educational leader for New Kent County and Hopewell City schools. She served eight years in the principalship and thirteen years as the director of mathematics, science, and technology for Hopewell Public Schools.

She has been an avid member of the John Tyler Community College Board of Visitors (Now Brightpoint Community College) for eight years and a lifetime member of the Virginia Association of Science Teachers, past president of the Charles City County NAACP and Civic League, and a lifetime member of the NAACP. Areas of interest are K–8 mathematics, transient and students at the Promise, poverty, leadership, instruction, coaching-instructional feedback, STEM, and lesson study.

She is one of the founding members of the Charles City Democratic Committee and serves as treasurer/vice president. She has spoken for various organizations and churches emphasizing educational and women's issues throughout Virginia.

Yvonne has been an adjunct instructor at the University of Virginia, Virginia Commonwealth University, Virginia State University, Regent University, and Mary Baldwin University. Yvonne is the director and CEO of Highly Effective Services, Inc. She has conducted numerous workshops for school divisions and conferences throughout Virginia, North Carolina, and Washington, D.C.

Volunteering is one of the most meaningful aspects of her life, and she takes part in numerous organizations such as Habitat for Humanity, Feedmore (Charles City Storehouse Promise), tutoring, STEM, and participating in the Cap to Cap Bike Trail, Susan G. Komen, and Relay for Life (cancer).

Overcoming Toxic Work Environments

DR. MYRIA D. THOMPSON

Stepping officially into adulthood came with much excitement, fear, and a sense of "freedom" for me once graduating from college. My first salaried position was as an elementary school teacher. Wow, was I thrilled and excited—ready to implement everything I'd learned to expand the young minds I was assigned to.

Out of all the topics covered while attending my higher learning institution—from educational pedagogy to reading—the one topic that was not covered was toxic work environments. However, one should not expect this to be a course offered, but at some point in our work experience, we may encounter such environments. This could have been only for a season. There are also those who may have never worked in unpleasant spaces, and that is a blessing.

However, the purpose of this chapter is to share my own experiences and how I overcame these workplaces and how it shaped me as a leader. My goal is also to provide practical biblical steps on how you, too, can overcome these environments should you ever find yourself in one or if you are currently in one. As Kingdom citizens, our growth does not stop within the walls of the church. It occurs on the outside of the church, wherever you may be.

As a young woman, I did not make this connection as I was experiencing various situations within my workplace. Oh, if I could turn back the hands of time, I would have approached and responded differently. However, this is how we grow and become better. The areas that I would like to explore that I believe are the most prevalent within a toxic workplace are gossipy work environments and toxic leadership.

GOSSIPY WORK ENVIRONMENTS

Who doesn't deal with gossip within the workplace? Who doesn't deal with gossip in everyday life? We are inundated and entertained with this toxic behavior as demonstrated from social media to "reality" television. Basically, salacious gossip sells and generates likes and hearts. There is no way around it because it's everywhere and has become so acceptable that our young children even indulge in it. Just look at the amount of online cyberbullying occurring. By definition, *Cyberbullying includes sending, posting, or sharing negative, harmful, false, or mean content about someone else* (Stopbullying.gov). The root to all this is gossip. Now, if young children are already becoming proficient and tech savvy in spreading gossip, what would their workplace look like by the time they come of age? That is a scary thought.

It's no surprise this behavior filters into the workplace, and we are all guilty of it. What seems like innocent banter about someone else is really damaging, not only to them, but the ones who are sharing the information. We often justify sharing the news because it may be true; however, the biblical scriptures are very clear about carrying such news and how to deal with those who carry it. Proverbs 20:19 aptly states, *"Whoever goes about slandering reveals secrets; therefore, do not associate with a simple babbler."* Ouch!

The Word refers to a gossiper as a simple babbler! Let that sink in. I recall times where I allowed individuals to bring me salacious gossip, and I allowed them to just keep going on and on, trying not to offend them with my disinterest. However, when you know better, you do better—at least you are supposed to. What keeps one repeatedly indulging in the gossip concerning other people, especially as a person in leadership? Leadership sets the tone of the organization. Talking about others in a negative way to another person within the organization will eventually bring morale down and usher in distrust from the bottom up. I have witnessed this behavior in leadership where personal information was shared with others that was not very flattering. Of course the one in leadership told the other person in "confidence," but it spread throughout the building because each one told someone else in confidence.

I recall just feeling a high level of distrust toward the person and aimed to keep anything personal to myself. The level of gossip was so incredibly horrible within this particular workplace that I had to tell someone who was peddling gossip toward me that I didn't know anything they were talking about, which I didn't, and I was not interested in partaking of the conversation. It just made the workplace so uncomfortable to have someone spread lie after lie about other people, and no one ever shut them down.

In the following section, I want to empower you and share ways to overcome the gossip peddling within the workplace. You do not have to be part of this toxic behavior nor let it dominate your life.

STEPS TO OVERCOME GOSSIPY WORK ENVIRONMENTS

So, how does one effectively keep clear of this behavior and not allow it to infiltrate into your life? As a Kingdom citizen, are you bold enough to shut down conversation that is both destructive and damaging, whether the information is true or not? Here are some simple but effective steps to help you overcome such conversations.

Simply Keep It Moving

The breakroom or wherever workers gather can quickly turn into a gossip gala. It may seem obvious, but if you have found yourself sucked in, just don't allow yourself to be in a situation to listen to the slanderous conversation. Go the complete opposite direction.

Speak Up!

Gently explain to the one carrying the gossip that what they are indeed carrying gossip, and it really should not be discussed. This can be done in a discreet manner as to not embarrass the one with the derogatory information. This may or may not work, but just as the carrier was bold in disseminating the gossip, become even bolder in not receiving it. Don't allow yourself to become a dumping ground of toxic conversation that people feel they can release on you.

Change the Subject

When the conversation takes a noticeable turn into gossip land, change the conversation. Distracting and steering the conversation to something more positive and uplifting will often let the carrier know that you are not partaking in it and you want to chat about something else. However, be sure to utilize tact as someone could become highly offended you just highjacked their opportunity to share juicy gossip, especially if it's something they are accustomed to doing. Don't allow them to think this is your customary activity and steer it somewhere else.

Say Something Nice

When someone has something negative to say about another person, simply say something nice about them. Keep in mind, unless you live with the person being spoken of, you don't know what's really going on with them.

Don't Believe the Hype

At the end of the day, choose not to believe what is being shared. If you have gone through all the previous steps to no avail, don't believe the gossip. Simply put yourself in the shoes of the person being spoken of. Would you want someone peddling derogatory and false information about you? Or what if it's true? Would you want your business being passed around in such a manner? Of course not. As Kingdom citizens, let's normalize spreading the Gospel, not spreading gossip.

TOXIC LEADERSHIP

At some point, we all have worked for an organization that had various types of leadership to provide directives to those under their authority. Leadership is to provide continuity of the business or organization. With that comes a multitude of personalities.

After working now for nearly twenty years, I have encountered numerous types of leadership styles and personalities—some awesome, some not so awesome. Growing up, it was instilled in me to have respect for those who were older than me and those in some authority position, so I had a solid foundation on how to show respect to leadership as a child. However, once I became an adult and encountered leadership styles that were not desirable, I struggled with demonstrating my upbringing in that area. I did not know how to handle toxic leadership, leaving me feeling incredibly despondent.

It became a struggle to come to work daily. It became difficult to hold my peace when witnessing blatant injustice occurring and leadership seemed to be okay or just simply turned a blind eye to what was happening. These experiences caused my heart to become hardened. It would unfortunately take several of these occurrences for me to finally stop asking God, "Why me?' to instead asking God, "What is the lesson for me?"

Before I dive into what was revealed for my own growth, I

want to unpack what the traits of toxic leadership look like. The workplace is a space to engage with all types of people, and as Kingdom citizens, it's imperative to know what we are encountering and move accordingly.

The first example of toxic leaders is *the cold leader*. This leader's primary focus or goal is that the ends justify the means, whatever that is. It doesn't matter who gets hurt or wounded in the process, just if their goal was met. There is often very little compassion or empathy for others and even those who work directly under them in co-leadership positions. In our current culture, this seems to be almost the practiced norm.

The next type of leader is what I like to call *the diva leader*. Their posture is everyone around them within the workplace is solely there to serve them and to satisfy their own needs such as power, status, and greed. Your thoughts and ideas really don't matter if it doesn't align with this leadership style.

Another type of leader is *the attention seeker*. They absolutely crave personal glory and being noticed publicly. It matters not if they made any real contributions to a project that their employees worked hard to complete. This attention-seeking leader is going to take the credit for the outcome without acknowledgment of the people who are the true masterminds behind it.

The controlling leader has centralized control over everything and everyone under all circumstances. No one can do anything without this type of leader involved somehow.

Lastly, *the ruler leader* views the organization somehow as their own personal kingdom, and all assets are at their disposal.

Do these traits sound familiar? Have you experienced any of these types of leadership styles, or do you see yourself within one of these traits?

Over the years, I have held several positions—from a teacher, airman, customer service representative to an entrepreneur—and reflecting, I have encountered two of these toxic traits among leadership, and it was difficult to maneuver. As mentioned earlier, as a younger person, I did not make the connection that as Kingdom citizens, we grow and mature outside of the church walls. I just became defensive and angry at what I witnessed or personally experienced and would speak out in the harshest manner. However, once I stopped asking why and asked what is it I am to learn, that's when God began to teach me on how to endure the hard things and still represent the Kingdom of God.

It's incredibly important not to compromise your faith when faced with these leadership traits because it's your response to the situation that either brings glory to the

Kingdom or dishonor. We are the light that should shine bright in our workplaces.

Matthew 5:14 says, *"You are the light of the world. A city set on a hill cannot be hidden."* So once again, our lights don't just shine in church or at home, but within our workplace or business. I failed multiple times in my response to issues that came about from leadership with these traits. I was inevitably hiding my light.

I had to learn the hard way that it's okay not to say anything at all, but to truly be led by the Holy Spirit. That very leader you explode on could be the one the Holy Spirit wants you to lead to Christ. Or if you are in leadership, the employee you mishandle may be the one God wants you to witness to. We are living in times where people are coming to the Kingdom of Light outside the walls of the church, and we as God's representatives on earth must be ready at all times to bring the message of salvation to anyone at any time.

In all these experiences, I had to learn how to lead people and how not to lead people. It was incredibly humbling, but I was determined to not do to others what I witnessed as one in a leadership position. I had plenty of examples of how *not* to lead, but very few on how to lead.

STEPS TO OVERCOMING TOXIC LEADERSHIP

There are a multitude of ways to address overcoming toxic leadership traits as someone who works under their authority. There are many articles written about toxic leadership and how to deal with them. In this section, I will provide the Biblical perspective to overcoming.

The first step is to not react to the negativity. I know this is easier said than done, especially if the negativity is truly unpleasant. Our faces often speak before we open our mouths. As one who represents the Kingdom of God, displaying a pleasant attitude even when the leadership is not being pleasant releases the love and peace of God. Remember, we are the light of the world. When encountering people in leadership who are moody, rude, et cetera, it doesn't mean you have to be. I recall having a supervisor who would not even speak to certain people they didn't like, and it was incredibly obvious. It created such a thick tension in the building that could literally be cut with a knife. I made it a point to not get on their "naughty" list as to not experience their wrath of passive aggression.

In the Biblical scriptures, Jesus compares us to salt. Matthew 5: 13 says, *"You are the salt of the earth. But if the salt loses its saltiness, how can it be made salty again?"* When examining the attributes of salt, when applied to food, it's supposed to make it taste better, and it also preserves food. As a Kingdom citizen, are we making things better in the workplace, or are we contributing to the toxicity? Are we preserving peace, our integrity, character, righteousness, love, or hope? Are we transforming the workplace, or are we conforming?

This does not mean to not follow directives and become disrespectful but to stand for righteousness. We have the unique ability to be positive change agents within the workplace.

As a leader, seek out someone to mentor you if you see yourself reflected in one of these toxic traits. Accountability is key to overcoming, and having someone walk beside you to show your blind spots is incredibly beneficial. The truth may hurt, but that happens when you grow and mature.

"As iron sharpens iron, so one person sharpens another."
-Proverbs 27:17

Attending and investing in leadership classes is also valuable as not many in leadership roles have taken courses that will assist in leading others. Learning how to lead other people, especially from a Biblical worldview can be invaluable.

Be quick to hear and slow to speak. It's always wise to be one of few words but allow the wisdom of God to direct and speak for you. I love what the Book of Proverbs 18:2 says about this: *"A fool takes no pleasure in understanding, but only in expressing his opinion"* (ESV). We live in a culture where the clap back is required and normalized as a response to something said to us that we don't like. No one wants to be viewed as being weak or looked at as a doormat to be walked on.

CONCLUSION

To end, overcoming toxic workplaces is achievable. We have the biblical pattern to do so. It does not matter where you work, as Kingdom citizens, we have a responsibility to represent Jesus here on earth. In the workplace environment, we are to be the light on the hill as reflected within the Biblical scriptures. We should not allow societal norms to dictate to us on how to handle toxic work environments.

Taking issues to social media seems to be the most popular response to things we don't like at work. Just type in workplace drama and look at the plethora of videos that people post. As we continue to live and work in various places or own businesses, it's our responsibility to lead and be led with Biblical worldview. Our response to leadership that is toxic should not mirror what the world does. Our standard is the Bible. The scriptures are clear that we will experience various trials and tribulations in life. This includes your place of business as a leader or one who is being led. However, we know that we have the victory, and we have confidence that we are overcomers.

I have learned many valuable lessons throughout the years while working in leadership and as one under leadership. I failed some, but I was also victorious in some. I had to trust the Holy Spirit to lead and teach me, even when it hurt. I encourage you to allow the Holy Spirit to lead and guide you on your job when situations become unbearable and tough. It's a blessing to be able to lead others, and as a leader, you are a reflection of the business or organization. What you allow to occur will filter down to those in the organization, thus creating an environment with high morale or low morale.

I pray this chapter has blessed you and that you continue in your respective leadership role or your desire to be a leader and that you move forward with a Kingdom perspective.

ABOUT THE AUTHOR

Dr. Myria Thompson originally hails from Oklahoma but has called Virginia her home since 1999. She is the wife of Robert B. Thompson III and the mother of Ethan N. Thompson. With a zeal for teaching, she has been a public educator for the past seventeen years, working with students with special needs. Dr. Myria is a lifelong learner and has traveled all over the United States taking classes as well as overseas attending the University of Haifa in Israel to study the Hebrew language.

Dr. Myria is an ordained minister and loves to serve people and has taken that love and started NUVISION Coaching where she is passionate about seeing people healed, delivered, and set free to walk into their God-given purpose. She and her husband are co-directors of the Healing Rooms of Petersburg, Virginia, which serves the community and is open for all to come and receive prayer and the love of Jesus.

Know Your Value and Squash Your Fear

KRISTINA P. TRUELL

It was a sunny spring day, and I was in Richmond to meet a friend for brunch. As we walked through her neighborhood toward the restaurant, I marveled at my friend's enthusiasm as she greeted each person she encountered and surprisingly, her energy was reciprocated. When I commented on how friendly the community was, she replied, "That's just what we do here." I recognized that it was more than that. She was genuinely open to connecting with other people and was purposeful about it. Her confidence and bold character became more evident when we were seated in the restaurant.

My friend sat next to two young ladies enjoying coffee martinis. By the time our drinks came, my friend had learned their names, where they'd gone to school, their professional roles, and was asking questions about their next career moves. Who can do that in less than five minutes? Mary. She is fearless, strategic, and bold! After all, she is an entrepreneur, and those character traits have led to success in business and adventure in her personal life. Mary has been invited to some of the more prestigious venues in the country and has been afforded opportunities that other vendors in her profession have not been offered because of her willingness to step out in boldness. Her *reason* for stepping out is simply, "If I don't sell, I don't eat."

As I think about the character and practice of other courageous women whom I have encountered, three themes emerge. Each of us understands our assignment, knows our value, and has learned to overcome our fears. I have been in education for twenty-three years and served as a teacher, building administrator, and now district administrator. My goal has been to transform classroom instruction so that students learn skills by participating in meaningful real-world experiences. As I have progressed in my career, I have learned to value my unique talents and gifts and developed the passion to encourage others to know their worth and value their successes.

BRAND-NEW TEACHER

In August 2000, I accepted a job as a teacher. I was a career switcher, coming from a career in sales management. To prepare for my new role, I read and studied classroom management and learned about pedagogy. I listened to those who shared, "Don't smile until December" and others who espoused building relationships with students. Others advised dressing in a suit and heels to give the look of authority, while others warned against looking too authoritarian. I was perplexed. What was the "right" way to show up and do the work?

Advice regarding classroom culture and environment was also plentiful. I was told students should be quiet, always on-task, seated in rows facing the teacher. The teacher, not the student, was the "sage" on the stage. Determined to succeed in my new role, I attempted to follow the advice I was given. I was miserable! But when I observed my colleagues, they were making it work in their classrooms. I tried again and again. I was still miserable and felt like a failure.

One day a veteran teacher pulled me aside after noticing my frustration. He told me to do something so simple that it changed my practice as a teacher. He said, *"When you close your door, it's your world, and you have to make it work for you."*

I was following someone else's script for teaching and learning. It didn't matter how I delivered the lessons as long as learning took place. This was the first time that I stepped out with boldness. We—teacher and students—worked together to set up the classroom the way that made sense to us. I entrusted the students to put together iMac computers, and they taught me the latest dances.

Students learned the home row keys—*ASDF JKL*—participated in typing races, and learned workplace skills. The classroom was loud, with lessons often led by students. It was a place of mutual respect and understanding.

Needless to say, the arrangement wasn't perfect, but I was willing to do the work. I chose to show up as my authentic self, dressed in a suit, pearls, heels, and committed to creating meaningful experiences for students in a keyboarding class.

A few years later, I was given the opportunity to teach business management and accounting. I was learning that my preferred teaching method was to use projects and authentic hands-on experiences. I found a program that incorporated authentic entrepreneurial and business management experiences while exposing students to living independently and managing their personal finances. There were a lot of moving parts to the program that required a lot of coordination. There was an executive team, marketing and finance departments, production team, and a bank that received payroll checks and placed funds into accounts from which "employees" paid their fixed and variable personal expenses. The students learned multiple aspects of business through problem-solving and active participation.

The process was messy. There were times when students sat on desks wondering what to do next and became frustrated because they were not given the "right" answer. Teams and departments changed over time as students discovered their strengths and interests. What a way to learn business management and accounting! Hands-on, trial and error, reflection, and collaboration in a student-centered environment. I was the facilitator, and students controlled the learning process.

My colleagues often wondered what my class was doing. There was laughter, loud voices, and music playing as students worked in their teams and made decisions about their products, services, and marketing strategy. The culminating activity was a virtual trade show in which students showcased their business and marketed their products with 135 other student-created businesses in a regional event.

I was proud of the transformation of this group. More importantly, the students too were proud of their accomplishments. They learned concepts in an engaging way and developed a confidence I'd not seen before. I took a risk to expose students to a non-traditional approach to instruction, and it paid off. I boldly transformed my teaching and their learning experience.

STAND YOUR GROUND

In 2008, I transferred to another school district whose demographic and culture were quite different. Most classrooms were structured with students sitting in rows and listening to teachers lecture. I took several bold steps to actively engage all adolescent learners in developing employability skills. Business marketing students showcased products they developed in a school-wide mock vendor trade fair. Students worked with area business partners to pitch business ideas and develop business plans. The same business partners were enlisted to judge displays and student professionalism. My greatest reward was watching reluctant students learn about business development and market their products in a confident, professional manner. They applied the skills learned in this non-traditional experience and learned some things about themselves along the way. Another set of students learned business and marketing concepts by creating and operating a school store. The students decided on the inventory, promotions, and managed and evaluated student workers. This endeavor allowed students to experience firsthand the effects of their decision making.

Career Technical Education provides access for all. Students with hearing impairments were encouraged to participate in the career investigations class. Teaching and learning was reciprocal. The students with hearing impairments learned about different careers and taught sign language to non–hearing impaired students. Active learning, fun, and mutual respect characterized the classroom.

TESTED AND PROVED

One summer I was asked to sit on an interview panel for the new assistant principal. The last candidate entered the room quietly and held on to a worn three-ring binder. She answered the questions succinctly yet with enough detail to let the panel know that she was passionate about the well-being and future success of all students. She was hired. Her "why" was doing what was best for all students, and she boldly challenged static systems and instructional practices that solely benefited teachers.

As I watched her, she was watching me. One day she came into my classroom with a flyer advertising a new administration and supervision cohort. She laid it on my desk and simply said, "Think about it."

What? Me, a building administrator? No way!

I watched the way teachers responded to administrators when they wanted something or when something didn't go their way. And what about parents and dealing with discipline issues on a daily basis? Nope!

She came back, and I was prepared to give all the reasons why I did not want to be an administrator. Before I could say anything, she asked me one question: "What is your career goal?"

I responded with, "My dream job is to become a CTE director."

"Good," she responded. "This is the first leg of the journey.

Fill out the application, and I will write your reference," and with that she was out of the room.

I filled out the application, was accepted into the program, and eighteen months later, I completed the program. In 2014, I accepted a high school assistant principal position.

The first months as a building administrator tested my abilities and made me question my decision to accept the offer. My type-B, accommodating self was exhausted and mentally drained from trying to keep up with all of the discipline issues, learning to supervise adults, and responding to situations in ways that pleased everyone. Frankly, I upset a lot of people, internalized less-than thinking, and spent late nights and weekends trying to stay afloat.

The stress damaged my body, and the unrelenting effort to get it right damaged precious relationships.

God sent people to separate me from destructive behaviors. They stepped out in boldness and influenced me to set boundaries, prioritize my well-being, and cultivate more authentic relationships with my *why*, my role, and myself. The experience showed me that I can never be all things to all people, and I will disappoint some people some of the time, and I have to be okay with it. The advice I received remains with me today: "As long as you can look at yourself in the mirror and say that you've done your best with the information and circumstances you received, it was a good day."

While I am still relationship-oriented, as a leader, I have had to expand my capacity to balance the needs of the "business" with my *why* and my boundaries. Letting go of my superwoman cape was challenging yet liberating. Any time I feel stress or confusion, I get quiet and reflect on my passion, my abilities, and the resources that I control. Focus and reflection calm my inner turmoil and allow me to move forward on purpose. Oftentimes boldness is a personal victory.

NEXT LEVEL

After my second year as an assistant principal, I began to get my groove. As a building leader, I learned and led discussions about accommodations, modifications, differentiation, and enrichment in special education, gifted instruction, English, and Math. I developed a passion for special education and differentiated instruction and was contemplating adding a special education endorsement to my credentials when I learned of an opening for CTE director.

Since becoming a CTE teacher, my dream was to become a CTE director, but now? I hesitated to apply because I felt that I still had work to do in my current role. To add, I was nominated and accepted into the Aspiring Special Education Leaders Academy. Timing is everything, and I was feeling conflicted. Perhaps what I was really feeling was anxiety about moving into a new role. I did the only thing I knew to do. I prayed and meditated on a familiar scripture, 2 Timothy 1:7: *"For God hath not given us the spirit of fear; but of power, and of love, and of a sound mind* (KJV)."

Less than a week later, I was seated in front of a five-person interview panel. I will never forget the experience. It was the first time that I ever felt fully at ease responding to interview questions. Typically, nervous energy would cause me to stumble over my responses to questions, but I remained poised and confident. I surprised myself while I marveled at God working in me—another personal victory achieved because I boldly stepped out on faith, confident in my purpose, and without fear.

STEPPING OUT OF MY COMFORT ZONE

Now what? As the supervisor of Career and Technical Education, my role is to oversee programs, services, and experiences that prepare students for careers after high school. I work with teachers, administrators, counselors, and businesses to expand learning experiences for students. When the COVID pandemic closed schools in March 2020, I was completing my third year in the role. Like everyone else, I isolated myself in my home, created an office space, and learned to communicate electronically. After a while, I realized that I could work from anywhere and packed up and went to spend time with my family in Pennsylvania. It was eerie driving from Virginia on interstate highways that were typically jammed with traffic. Nonetheless, if I had to be isolated, I wanted to be with people that I loved.

My five-day trip turned into a two-week staycation at my sister's home with my brother-in-law, nephews, son, and my mother. We all had different places in the house where we connected with work and school via Zoom. The front porch was the gathering spot for evening meals on the grill, adult beverages, music, and fun.

It was a peaceful and carefree time—until the George Floyd incident. There were riots in the streets of Philadelphia and protests on I-95 in Delaware. Even in our peaceful retreat, we were overcome with outrage while experiencing the sadness of lives lost to COVID. It was an emotional time.

When I returned to Virginia, I was saddened by the damage and windows boarded up on Broad Street and neighboring areas. The school division leadership team was called back to work to prepare for the upcoming school year shortly after the horrific death of George Floyd. Everyone started talking about diversity, equity, and inclusion (DEI), including my school division. In a Zoom meeting, the facilitator attempted to provide a space for the leadership team to express their thoughts and feelings about the current racial tensions and DEI.

I was distracted. No one had their cameras on, and I became overwhelmed with the black tiles with the names of the participants in white letters. An overwhelming sadness weighed heavy on me, and I sobbed uncontrollably. I tried to gather myself, but I couldn't. I reached out to a Black male co-worker who I admired for *keeping it real*. I needed help to make sense of what I was feeling. He spoke softly but could offer no words to comfort me. I realized that he too was experiencing similar emotions. When I got off the phone with him, the image of the black tiles loomed in my mind. I had to do something!

Then I remembered what a minister declared to me just months before the pandemic: "They are waiting for you to move them forward." I made up my mind to meet with the superintendent to tell her that I wanted to lead the DEI work the division was planning.

This was a bold move for me because now I would be pushed into the forefront when I am quite comfortable providing support from the background and I knew little about effectively implementing a DEI plan. I didn't think about my personal comfort, only that there was work to be done, and I wanted to make sure it got done—or at least started. In August of 2020, I gave my initial presentation to the division leadership team to launch the Diversity, Equity, and Inclusion initiative.

Again, I focused on the assignment, and I had a strong inclination that I had the skills and sensibilities to launch the DEI initiative. More importantly, I squashed my fear.

FINAL THOUGHTS

"In all the years I've known her, I have *never* heard her sing. That chick has a beautiful voice." These words were exclaimed by my best sister-friend. We were in a *room* on Clubhouse, a social audio app where users can communicate in audio chat rooms that accommodate groups of people from anywhere in the world. The room, Walking In the Spirit Prayer Room, is dedicated to daily prayer and inspirational teachings.

This day the men and women in the room were asked to pray aloud for one another. When I heard the instructions, I became anxious, nervous to pray amidst pastors, evangelists, and others more skilled at prayer than I. As the participants in the room began to pray, I recognized my trepidation betrayed my practice. Fear is my imagination trying to keep me from moving. I squashed it!

I kept hearing my new favorite tune and felt prompted to sing. *What? Sing in public?* I said to myself. Every muscle tightened in my jaws, shoulders, and back. I just talked myself into praying, and now I am being led to sing. *Exhale!* Several thoughts quickly entered my mind and immediately put me at ease. I recognized the *Why* of the prayer, and I acknowledged my passion for my new favorite song and its significance to me. More importantly, I pushed past the fear that I was inadequate. I sang and prayed with confidence and boldness.

My thoughts: You can't serve anyone by shrinking into the background. Know your worth, show up, and crush the fear!

ABOUT THE AUTHOR

Kristina Truell was born and raised near Philadelphia, Pennsylvania, the home of cheesesteaks, hoagies, and her beloved Philly sports teams. She is an educator championing career readiness and a new co-author of *Influencers Stepping Out in Boldness*. Kristina considers her faith, her *tribe*, and encouraging others to be important aspects of her life. She strives to help others use their gifts and hopes that her influence changes their path in significant ways.

Intimate Advocacy

DANA D. WILSON

"God grant me the serenity to accept the things
I cannot change, the courage to change the things I can,
and the wisdom to know the difference."

I was introduced to this prayer as a young girl. The Serenity Prayer simply means letting go of situations beyond your control and taking action toward things within your control. This has shown to be the mantra of my life.

Can I really do something to influence or impact this situation or circumstance in any way? Interestingly enough, in most cases, I believe I can. So, I will attempt different angles or approaches then examine the positive or negative effects of my efforts. Either way, I rely on God to speak to my spirit to let it go or continue to pursue. This method ultimately has served me well over the years. I have always been a lover of learning. Exploring history, learning new things, and being open to consider new concepts is fun for me.

Most importantly, I love to share the exciting new news with others. It is my duty and purpose to share with others so they too can gain from the discoveries. This has landed me in tough spots, new spaces, and led to intimate advocacy.

THE SISTERLOCKS LIFESTYLE

"This is it! This is exactly what I need for my life."

This is what I whispered to myself while surfing the internet at work. I so happened to come across a small hyperlink www.sisterlocks.com in late 1999. I was in shock and awe of the mere audacity that it could be possible to embrace my natural texture of my hair and it be styleable, manageable, beautiful, and look acceptable to the masses. This notion was life changing. By January 2000, I was walking tall in my very own Sisterlocks. The freedom I was experiencing fueled me to become a Sisterlocks consultant to share this new discovery with others with tightly textured hair. The Sisterlocks lifestyle was more than just hair. This was therapeutic, this was a Black hair movement, this was acceptance of oneself.

God positioned and postured me to escort others through this transition of self-discovery and full self-expression by way of hair. How you feel about yourself in your skin and when you look in the mirror is intimate and determines how you show up in the world. It has been an honor, privilege, and pleasure to play a role in hundreds of intimate journeys to natural hair freedom. There have been many intimate journeys that the Lord has seen fit that I be a partner to. My track record indicates there will be many more matters to advocate for in the future.

SPECIAL NEEDS

My son, Landon, has been labeled special needs. The worldly definition of special needs refers to individuals who require assistance for disabilities that may be medical, mental, or psychological. Landon has short bowel syndrome and falls on the autism spectrum. It has been an interesting ride learning of the various specialists and therapists that exist. Each of their disciplines work together to make up a wellness and developmental plan created specifically for him.

My experience in Landon's world has given me an epiphany: We all are special needs to a certain degree. Maybe it's not to an extreme, but we all have special needs medically, mentally, and psychologically unique to us as individuals. We just naturally curate our own support systems around our special needs. Our family, choices of friends, mates, affiliations, and communities tell the story of our needs. Landon has been a blessing. For some reason, much earlier in my son's journey, I knew it was not just for me but for many families to benefit. I advocate daily on our behalf for services, learn new modalities, stay abreast of new treatments, and research technologies and adaptive equipment.

I've come to realize that embracing each other and understanding that we are ordinary people who can do extraordinary things can be the gateway to supporting people to living out their full potential. How can I say this? Well, it's been my observation that people who accept and embrace their special needs family members and lean into their strengths and seek support to adapt to the challenges often get breakthroughs. They seek and search for the right combination that opens doors.

Understanding ordinary people can do extraordinary things keeps us present to our power. Therefore, you have no real limitations, just a jigsaw puzzle to put together and complete.

HAIR LOSS

Over my twenty-plus years as a Sisterlocks wearer, consultant, trainer, and coach, I've observed hair loss firsthand. I was a witness and experienced for myself the emotional toll of watching your crown and glory fading away. I learned hair loss (alopecia) is simply a disruption of the hair life cycle. Although simply stated, it's not that simple to find the root cause. This is an intimate journey to find out your "why."

As a young girl, I was always intrigued with why. Why did the sun rise in the morning and set at night? Why do people think the way they do? Why did someone create this thing, way, and/or place? Then next I pondered the how. How does this work? How can I use this? How come not many people know about this? Well, all that curiosity came back to the surface around hair loss. I learned there are so many factors that could contribute to why you lose hair such as diet, hormonal imbalance, vitamin deficiencies, inflammation, and autoimmune disorders. Also, stress can exacerbate your hair loss.

So, there is some of the whys. Now the hows to rejuvenate your scalp and regenerate new hair is easier said than done. This is not to scare you, but to get you prepared for the 3 Cs that it takes to fight for every strand.

3 CS—COMMITMENT, COMPLIANCE, CONSISTENCY

Commitment

Commitment is a promise or pledge to do something with a

high level of dedication and determination. It's making a conscious decision to stick with something, even when it's challenging, and to put in the effort needed to achieve a desired outcome.

Compliance

Compliance is adherence to standards or guidelines established for ultimate results. It is important because it helps to ensure you do things in accordance with the protocols established, which promotes safety and accountability.

Consistency

Consistency refers to the quality of being consistent or reliable in behavior, attitudes, and actions over time. It involves the ability to maintain stable and predictable approaches to act in a way that aligns with goals. It is important to perform at a high level consistently over time to see results.

The idea that you could possibly stop and slow down hair loss and intentionally regenerate new hair is fascinating, challenging, and personal to me. My hair advocacy has now evolved into becoming a certified trichologist. I stand to support people like myself who may suffer from a scalp disorders and/or hair loss issues. This quest to learn more has resulted in that it takes piecing mind, body, and spirit components together to fight for every strand. I would highly suggest the following wholistic approach of the utilizing the 3 C's with these areas of care:

- Circulation
- Stimulation
- Exfoliation
- Elimination
- Nutrition
- Hydration
- Supplementation
- Oxygenation
- Meditation
- Relaxation
- Detoxification

In no certain order of superiority, all components work together for our good. I know you are probably thinking this is a lot, but you probably practice all components now, just not in a conscious, consistent, or intentional way. Remember, we all have special needs so the protocols, for scalp rejuvenation and hair regeneration is intimate and personal.

COACHING AND BUSINESS CONSULTING

When I began my Sisterlocks career, I had no business experience. In fact, I really did not have real plans to run a business. I just wanted to share the natural freedom I experience with others. I know that sounds silly, but it's true. I took the initial Sisterlocks consultant training, went home, and used my family to establish my first heads to practice. Boy, oh boy, did I have a rude awakening. It took hours and hours—sometimes days—to finish a head. Doing Sisterlocks and the freedom of wearing them was two different things. You had to consider so many variables to provide personal service to each client. I was determined to follow through and wanted to be great for the result for the client.

I tried reaching out to other consultants to get continual education. However, the pool of consultants was not as plentiful as it is now. My next course of action was to take an official refresher course. It was there that I could ask educated questions because of my little experience. The refresher was helpful with technique, but it did not help with business management, time management, customer relations, client cultivation, marketing, and such.

I had never done business. Now, remember I begin my business as a sharer. Being an owner, operator, manager, marketer, and on active-duty military was a lot. Sisterlocks consulting was not my bread and butter at the time, but I still wanted to do a great job, provide a service, and be professional. I was flying by the seat of my pants. I did everything wrong to learn how to do it right. I learned a lot of do's and don'ts the hard way. I had to shift my mindset into minding my business and taking it seriously instead of just sharing the good news of Sisterlocks.

I eventually climbed the Sisterlocks ladder to certified consultant, R-certified, certified trainer associate, product distributor, certification evaluator, master trainer, brand ambassador, and Sisterlocks trichology analyst. Oh, how I loved the Sisterlocks lifestyle. I enjoyed training others in this one-of-a-kind natural haircare management system.

Well, then my life did a major shift the moment my son arrived. Of course I had to fall way back on the number of clients I could serve and classes I could train. My son required lots of love, energy, and time, so an untimely exit from the military was a must. Doing business had now become serious business. I had to get smarter, so I earned a bachelor's in business administration. This definitely took my business to the next level. I began implementing and aligning my processes, procedures, protocols, and policies that made sense to my unique business, lifestyle, and dreams. So here I go again, advocating for others to get coaching and business consulting.

Over the years, I would always mentor Sisterlocks trainees who reached out to me. But I had not formalized the manner in which I delivered. But once, I took stock and owned that the trainees working with me resulted in confidence, clarity, certification, clientele, and increased revenue, I knew what was next. The Hair Cares coaching train offers encouraging support, an accountability partner, and strategic planning to creating a business that supports your lifestyle and your dreams. Coaching is just a continuation of my pattern to learn something, experience it and share with others and then go learn some more. I just can't help myself. God designed me this way.

Every Strand Counts

Although I have been sharing my story, I know that my experience is not unique to me. I know that if you look back, the way you operate, the decisions and choices made stem from your core beliefs, prayer, and/or faith too. As a little girl, you could find me in my room reading. In fact, if you snuck up on me after bedtime, you might have found me under the covers with my flashlight reading a few more chapters of the book I was reading that I could not let go. I could not wait to share what I learned with family and friends because I had a knowing that my sharing could benefit, influence, and impact others.

This belief has ordered my steps. This behavior has charged me to be an intimate advocate. What does that really mean? Well, for some reason, God has presented real personal, intimate matters in my path. Whether it's advocating for services and treatments to support our special humans to be seen and heard, advocating for people with tightly textured hair to feel great about their God-given tresses, advocating for people who may be suffering in silence from a scalp disorder or hair loss to live wholistically and that there is hope, and advocating for natural hair practitioners to get coaching and consulting to build a business that complements their lifestyle from the onset, within every matter that God has called me to be an advocate, I have personal experience.

See, all your experiences, skills, and superpowers that you have gained over the years are transferable. They all count toward your life's purpose. The world is waiting on you to acknowledge, accept, and share. Someone is missing out because you have not shared yet. I am convinced if we share, encourage, and guide others to connect the dots of their lives, it can help people to get out of the quicksand of pity that we find ourselves in when we don't understand why we're going through or experiencing things. It really is for others too.

Sharing our stories can touch, move, and inspire at least one person to connect their strands, own them, and stand upright in and with them. I encourage you to put your toe out there so God can help you with the rest. Let's be assured and reminded of God's word in Isaiah 41:13 (NLT): *"For I am the LORD your God, who takes hold of your right hand and tells you: Do not fear, I will help you."*

I will never forget listening to a commencement address where the speaker shared that you have a zero percent chance if you do not try. Man, you cannot shake the reality of what he shared: "God grant me the serenity to accept the things I cannot change, the courage to change the things I can and the wisdom to know the difference." I still stand by this mantra.

Here at Hair Cares Inc., our vision is to empower audacious women with an understanding that Every Strand Counts by piecing your mind, body, and spirit components together, which results in scalp rejuvenation, hair regeneration, and a growing, profitable, and sustainable Sisterlocks business.

- We provide in-person and virtual hair growth services, Sisterlocks business consulting and personal coaching and mentorship.

- We believe every strand counts. Every root, every lesson, every experience, and every legacy makes a difference in our lives.

- We are proud to encourage holistic living and full self-expression through hair advocacy, training, coaching, consulting, books, and our talk show *Every Strand Counts with Dana Wilson.*

Me, personally, I will die fighting and advocating. Fighting and advocating for love, to reach my goals, to live out my dreams, to be the best version of myself, and ultimately to win my own race.

ABOUT THE AUTHOR

Dana Wilson is a certified trichologist, Sisterlocks educator, empowerment coach, certified BIO research assistant, certified cold capper, veteran, author, and more importantly a mother of a son on the autism spectrum. She is the director and CEO of Hair Cares Inc., which provides in-person and virtual hair growth services, Sisterlocks business consulting, and personal coaching.

Dana's mission is to empower audacious women with an understanding that Every Strand Counts by piecing mind, body, and spirit components together, which results in scalp rejuvenation, hair regeneration, and a growing sustainable Sisterlocks business. She encourages holistic living and full self-expression through hair advocacy, training, coaching, consulting, books, and the talk show *Every Strand Counts.*

www.ingramcontent.com/pod-product-compliance
Lightning Source LLC
Chambersburg PA
CBHW051528120626
46551CB00012B/1130